THE
FLIGHT
BOOK

David Jefferis

RAINBOW

First published in 1992 by Rainbow Books,
Elsley House, 24-30 Great Titchfield Street,
London, W1P 7AD.

10 9 8 7 6 5 4 3 2 1

This book was included in The Flight Pack published in 1991 by Kingfisher Books.

© Grisewood and Dempsey Ltd 1991.

All rights reserved. No part of this publication may be reproduced, stored in a retrieval system or transmitted by any means, electronic, mechanical, photocopying or otherwise, without the prior permission of the publisher.

ISBN 1 87 1745 93 4

Printed in Hong Kong

Designed by David Jefferis
Edited by Gwen Edmonds
Illustrated by
Drawing Attention
Jeremy Gower
Mark Franklin
Michael Roffe
Robert and Rhoda Burns
Photographic credits
David Jefferis 2, 6, 7, 10, 11, 16, 29, 31, 35, 36
ZEFA 8, 9, 24, 26, 29; Quadrant 13;
Boeing 14, 30; AGE Fotostock 17, 39;
Air France 22; Lufthansa 27.

CONTENTS

The world of air travel	4
Flight city	6
Inside the terminal	8
Loading up	10
Inside the aircraft	12
On the flight deck	14
Permission for takeoff!	16
Into the air	18
Above the clouds	20
In flight	22
Enjoying the view	24
Approach and landing	26
Airport safety	28
Plane spotting	30
Time zones	34
Air facts	35
The story of airliners	36
Glossary	38
Index	40

THE WORLD OF AIR TRAVEL

❏ It's time to go on an air trip! When you first arrive at the airport, it can seem a confusing place. In fact, the hustle and bustle is carefully controlled, the aim being to get huge numbers of people through the airport as speedily as possible.

One of the world's busiest airports is Chicago's O'Hare in the USA. Over 55 million people use it every year, and there are nearly 70,000 aircraft movements (airport code for a takeoff or landing) each week, roughly one every 40 seconds or so.

Such airports are like cities, with fire and ambulance services, shops, restaurants and so on. London's Heathrow airport provides jobs for about 50,000 people, from floor cleaners to air traffic controllers.

DID YOU KNOW?

✓ Airports of the 1920s and 1930s had no concrete runways. All the small and light aircraft of the time needed was a flat grass field.

✓ Modern runways vary in length, but that of Doha airport in the Persian Gulf is one of the longest, at 4615 m (15,142 ft).

✓ Amsterdam's Schiphol airport, one of the busiest in Europe, is built on land reclaimed from the sea. It lies just below sea level.

▷ Aerial view of a typical airport. The most important buildings are the passenger terminals and the control tower. From here, controllers direct aircraft both on the ground and as they take off and land.

FLIGHT CITY

❑ There are lots of things to look out for at an airport. You should be able to see the control tower as you approach and often the fuel stores are visible too. Here, tanker trucks prepare to refuel the aircraft. Passengers' cars are left in car parks just outside the terminal itself.

Between the terminal buildings and the runway is the concrete apron, a wide flat area where the airliners park to unload, be refuelled, and be loaded up again. Most airports have a viewing area where you can watch this activity going on. It's well worth a visit if there is time before your flight.

▷ Huge windows in the futuristic terminal at Kennedy airport in New York reveal the sleek shapes of taxiing airliners beyond the glass.

Tail quiz

Airlines are very proud of their individual paint schemes and badges. Here are ten airliner tails. See if you can recognize the airlines concerned. The answers are on page 40. Tick the circle and mark in the date when you spot each one.

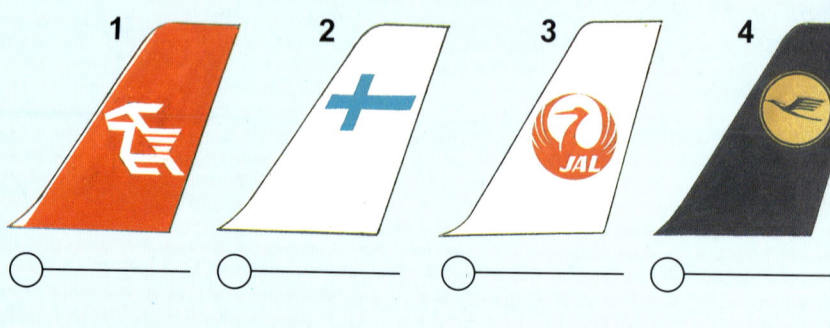

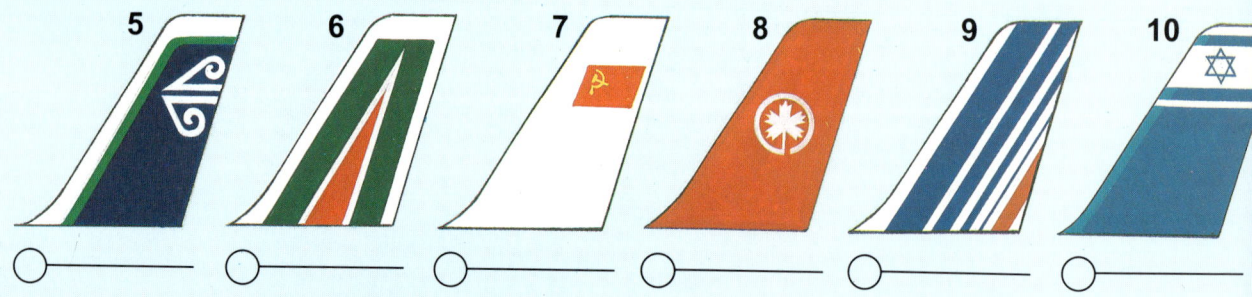

6

△ Heathrow airport in London is one of the world's busiest. When it opened for business in 1946 however, the best arrival and departure lounges it could offer its passengers were these ex-army tents!

▽ Airports large and small operate a similar system for ensuring a smooth flow of passengers and their baggage. The aim is always the same, to get people through the airport as quickly as possible.

Organizing the passengers and their bags

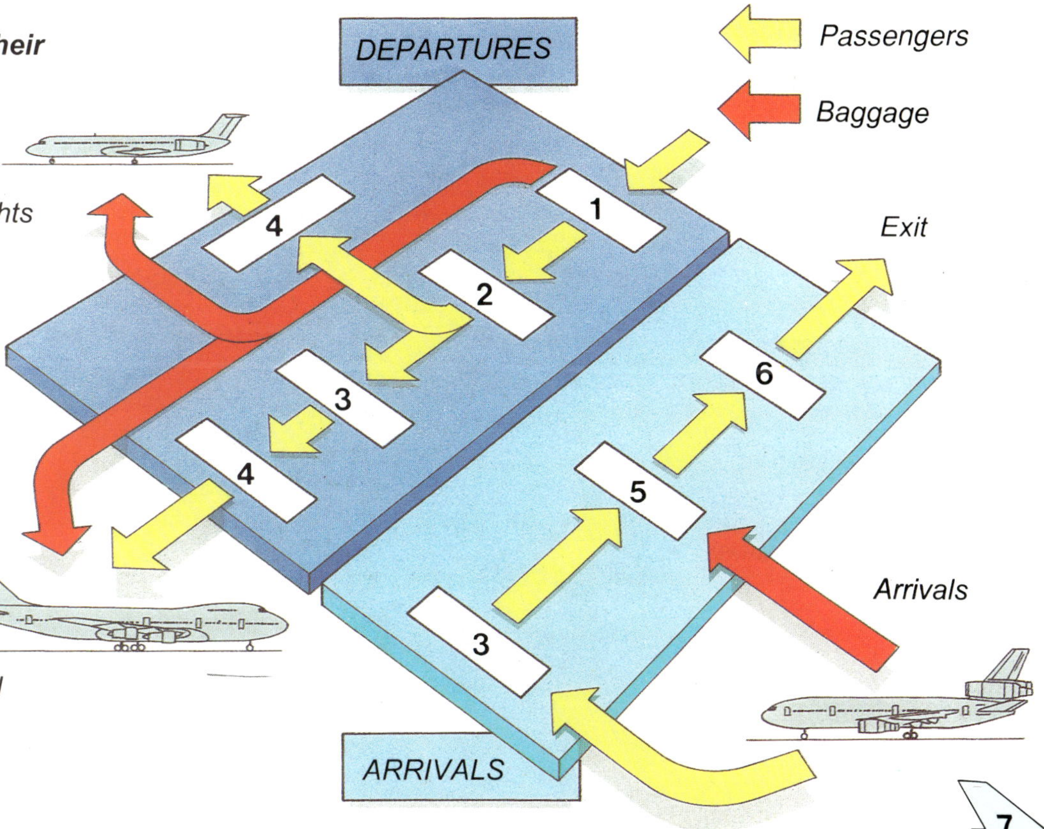

1 Check-in
2 Waiting areas
3 Passport checks
4 Security checks
5 Pick up bags
6 Customs checks

INSIDE THE TERMINAL

❑ The first thing to look out for when you pass into the departure terminal is your airline's check-in desk area. It is usually easy to find, but the smaller airlines often use the desks of bigger ones.

The check-ins themselves follow a similar pattern at all airports. They combine a desk and weighing scales for your bags. Once your flight ticket has been checked by the airline official, and your name added to the computerized passenger list, the bags are weighed and given a baggage tag. This tells the loaders which aircraft to put them on and your receipt should enable the airline to track them down if they should get lost.

△ You have to check in anything up to three hours before your flight leaves, depending on the airline. If you arrive late you won't have a good choice of seat, and might not get on at all.

The essential paperwork

These three tickets will get you aboard your plane – the air ticket, purchased beforehand; a boarding pass, given to you at check-in; a baggage tag for your suitcases. Passengers with only hand baggage will not need a baggage tag.

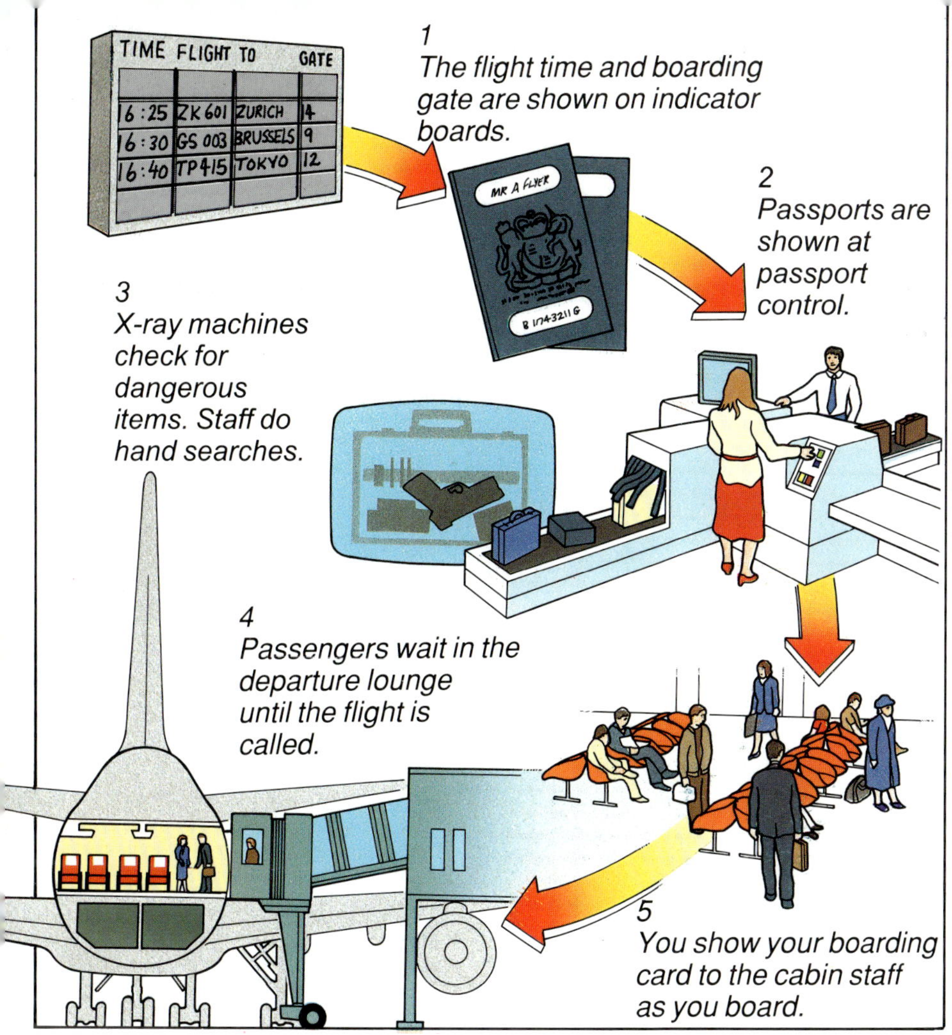

1 The flight time and boarding gate are shown on indicator boards.

2 Passports are shown at passport control.

3 X-ray machines check for dangerous items. Staff do hand searches.

4 Passengers wait in the departure lounge until the flight is called.

5 You show your boarding card to the cabin staff as you board.

◁ After check in, you go through to passport control and the departure lounge. Here and in the main terminal, flight details flash up on overhead indicator boards. As soon as your flight is shown, head towards the gate indicated. Gates are the exit points to the aircraft. At security control, you will normally be searched and your hand baggage put through an X-ray machine. In the departure lounge you wait again until your flight is called; then it's all aboard!

▽ The last check is the metal-detector. Magnetic fields reveal the presence of metal objects as you walk through.

▽ These are the essentials for any trip abroad.

HOLIDAY CHECKLIST

- Passport
- Any Visas
- Any Vaccinations
- Foreign Money
- Traveller's Cheques
- Property/Medical Insurance
- Air Ticket
- Maps and Guides
- Baggage Labels

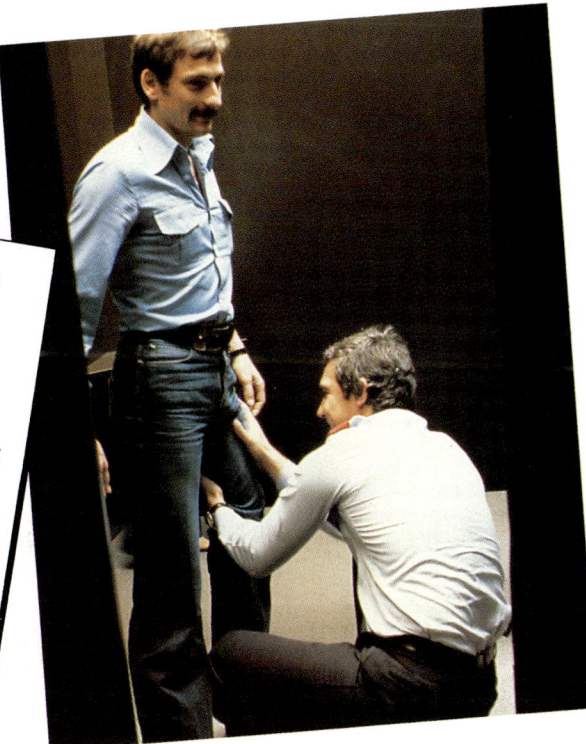

LOADING UP

Fuel tanker carries kerosene, a standard jetliner fuel

❑ An airliner has to spend as little time as possible on the ground, for it only earns its keep when carrying passengers. Immediately the aircraft is parked, trucks drive up and surround it, ready for loading and servicing.

Catering truck loads food and drink

Mobile stairs

Tug moves aircraft from its parking bay

Fuel tanker

Most aircraft can be turned around in under half an hour. While baggage trucks take away suitcases, others arrive with a new load. Toilets are cleaned and galleys restocked with food and drink. The aircraft's engines and systems are checked over by skilled technicians. At big airports kerosene aviation fuel can be pumped aboard by hydrant refuellers. These link to underground fuel pipes and can fill a plane's tanks in about 18 minutes. Big tankers are also used for the same job.

Cargo loader

Electrical services vehicle

△ A big fuel tanker, together with smaller hydrant pumping vehicles.

▽ A conveyor loads bags aboard a jet. Bulk cargo is carried in containers.

◁ Mobile lounges carry people direct to the planes at Montreal in Canada.

△ This truck has a 'scissors' action to hoist its load to the aircraft doors.

11

INSIDE THE AIRCRAFT

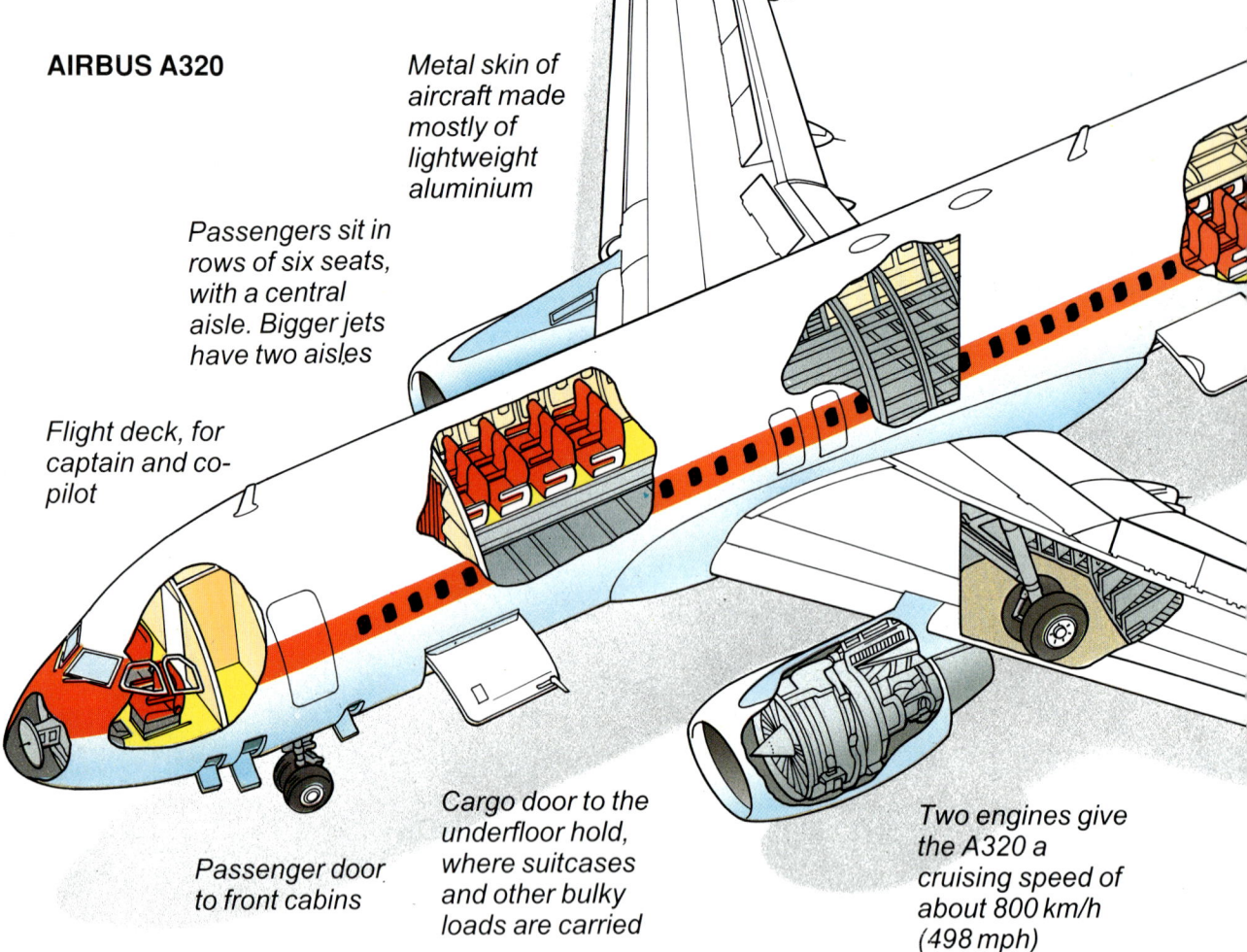

AIRBUS A320

Metal skin of aircraft made mostly of lightweight aluminium

Passengers sit in rows of six seats, with a central aisle. Bigger jets have two aisles

Flight deck, for captain and co-pilot

Passenger door to front cabins

Cargo door to the underfloor hold, where suitcases and other bulky loads are carried

Two engines give the A320 a cruising speed of about 800 km/h (498 mph)

❏ Your jet airliner is the result of spectacular progress in aviation design. In the 1930s, few planes could carry more than 20–30 passengers, and even by the 1950s, when the first jets went into service, there was room for no more than 100 or so people. Today, the biggest jets can carry four times this number in air-conditioned comfort.

The cabin layout of most modern airliners is fairly similar. In the nose section is the flight deck, where the captain and co-pilot sit. Behind them are the passenger cabins, running the length of the fuselage. Seats are laid out in rows, with aisles for you to walk along. First class passengers usually sit towards the front. They pay more for their tickets and get bigger seats and more comfort for their money.

You can usually find toilets at the front and rear, while on the bigger jets, the kitchen (called the 'galley'), where food and drinks are prepared for your in-flight meals, is usually in the centre section, between passenger cabins.

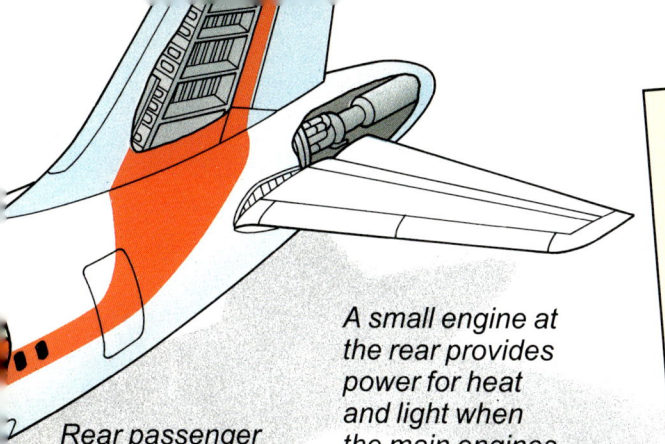

Rear passenger door

Rear cargo door

A small engine at the rear provides power for heat and light when the main engines are shut down at an airport

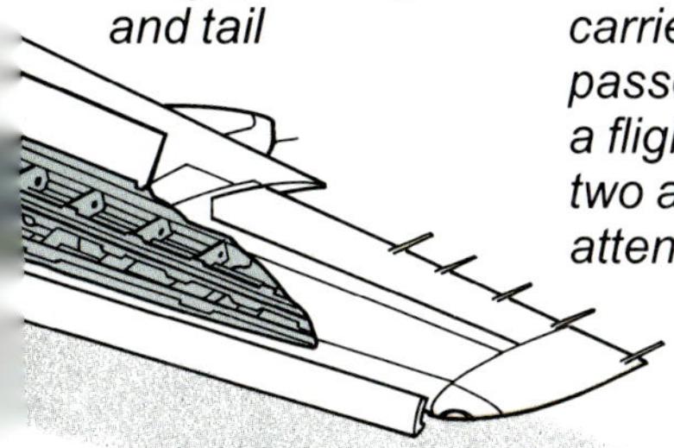

Fuel is carried in tanks in the wings, fuselage and tail

This Airbus A320 carries up to 180 passengers, with a flight crew of two and five cabin attendants

DID YOU KNOW?

✓ Much of the A320 is made of carbon fibre, a lightweight material stronger than metal.

✓ All flight controls on the A320 are controlled by computers.

✓ For a typical flight, a Boeing 747 carries over 156 tonnes of fuel, enough to keep a car on the road for four years.

△ Seats are carefully designed for comfort, but on long flights, even the most seasoned travellers need to get up and stretch their legs from time to time!

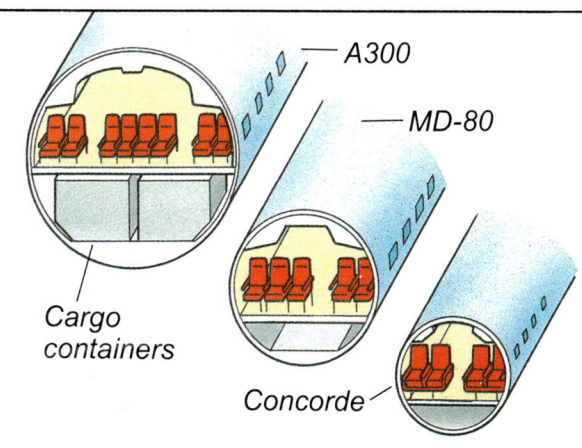

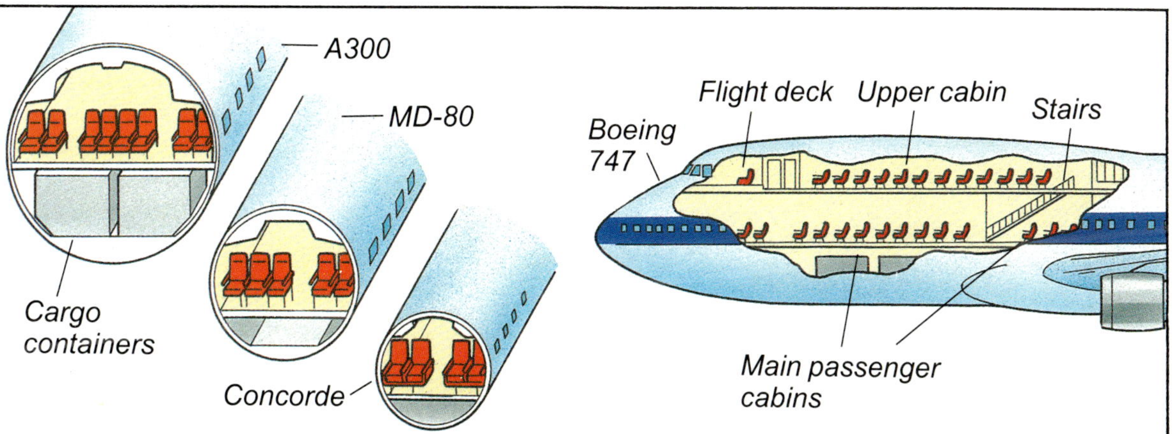

Seating arrangements depend largely on aircraft size. Smaller planes have four or five-abreast seating, while larger ones can have rows up to ten seats wide. The Boeing 747 has an extra cabin on the upper deck for first class passengers. Cargo and passengers' suitcases are carried under the main decks in specially-shaped containers, which are easy to load and unload.

13

ON THE FLIGHT DECK

❏ At first glance the flight deck cockpit is a bewildering mass of controls and instruments. But in fact, they fall into several easy-to-understand groups. In front of each seat (captain on the left, co-pilot to the right) is a control column for directing the aircraft. Foot pedals work the rudder. Directly in front of the seats are the flight instruments. These cover the basics, such as speed, height and angle of the plane. Between the seats are the engine instruments and throttle controls. Other equipment includes the radio and navigation instruments and the radar, which will warn of bad weather ahead.

On the latest jets, designers have replaced the traditional mechanical instruments with colour television screens. These mostly operate on the 'dark and quiet' rule, they display only what the crew need to know, and don't overload them with lots of minor details. Computerized cockpits have reduced the number of people needed to fly a jet. Early Boeing 747s had flight crews of five; the latest 747-400 needs only the captain and co-pilot.

▽ The flight deck of the Boeing 747-400 contains the latest digital TV instrument displays, which replace mechanical indicators used on earlier airliners.

Using the flight controls

The captain and co-pilot fly the plane using hand controls and foot pedals. The basics haven't changed since the early days of flying. Turning the control wheel from left to right moves small control surfaces on the wings called ailerons. These move up and down to roll the plane.

Pushing and pulling the control column moves tail surfaces called elevators. These move to pitch the plane up and down.

Pressing the rudder pedals moves the rudder. A plane flies naturally into a turn using just the ailerons, but the rudder is used for fine adjustments. On the ground, rudder pedals double as wheel brake controls.

Moving the control wheel sideways controls roll

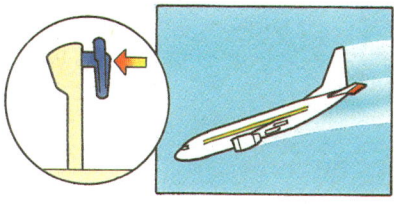 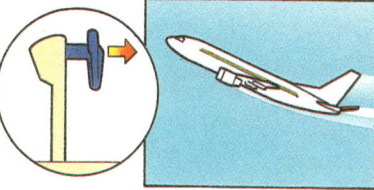

Pulling the wheel back and forward controls pitch

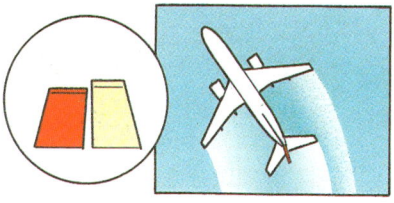 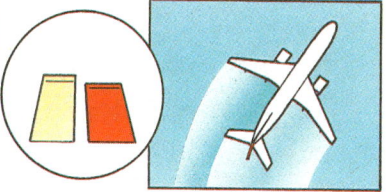

Pressing the rudder pedals controls turn

The flight instruments

Three of the most important instruments in the cockpit are the altimeter, air speed indicator and artificial horizon.

The altimeter indicates height above sea level. It measures air pressure, so does not show high ground, such as mountains.

The air speed indicator measures speed through the air. It doesn't measure ground speed, so a plane flying with a tail wind will be faster than one in still air, even though the indicator reading may be the same.

The artificial horizon shows whether the plane is in level flight or not, essential when flying at night or in cloud.

  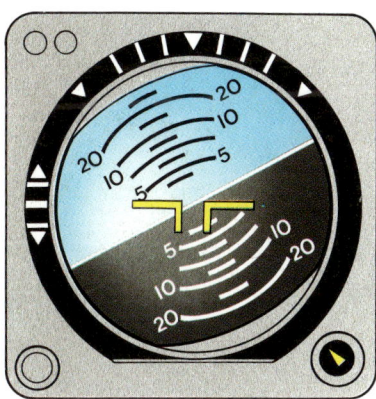

Altimeter   Air speed indicator   Artificial horizon

PERMISSION FOR TAKEOFF!

❏ Controllers in the tower are in charge of all aircraft movements. At the top of the tower is the visual control room which gives an all-round view of the airport. Controllers here are in charge of all takeoffs, taxiing and final landing instructions.

Below the visual control room are the radar controllers who scan the skies on radar screens for up to 80km (50 miles) around. Aircraft show up as small glowing blips, and it is the job of the controllers to direct all aircraft through their airspace in safety. They have to concentrate very hard and need a break every 90 minutes.

△ A Concorde taxies out towards the runway, ready for a transatlantic flight. The supersonic jet's crew are under orders from airport ground controllers.

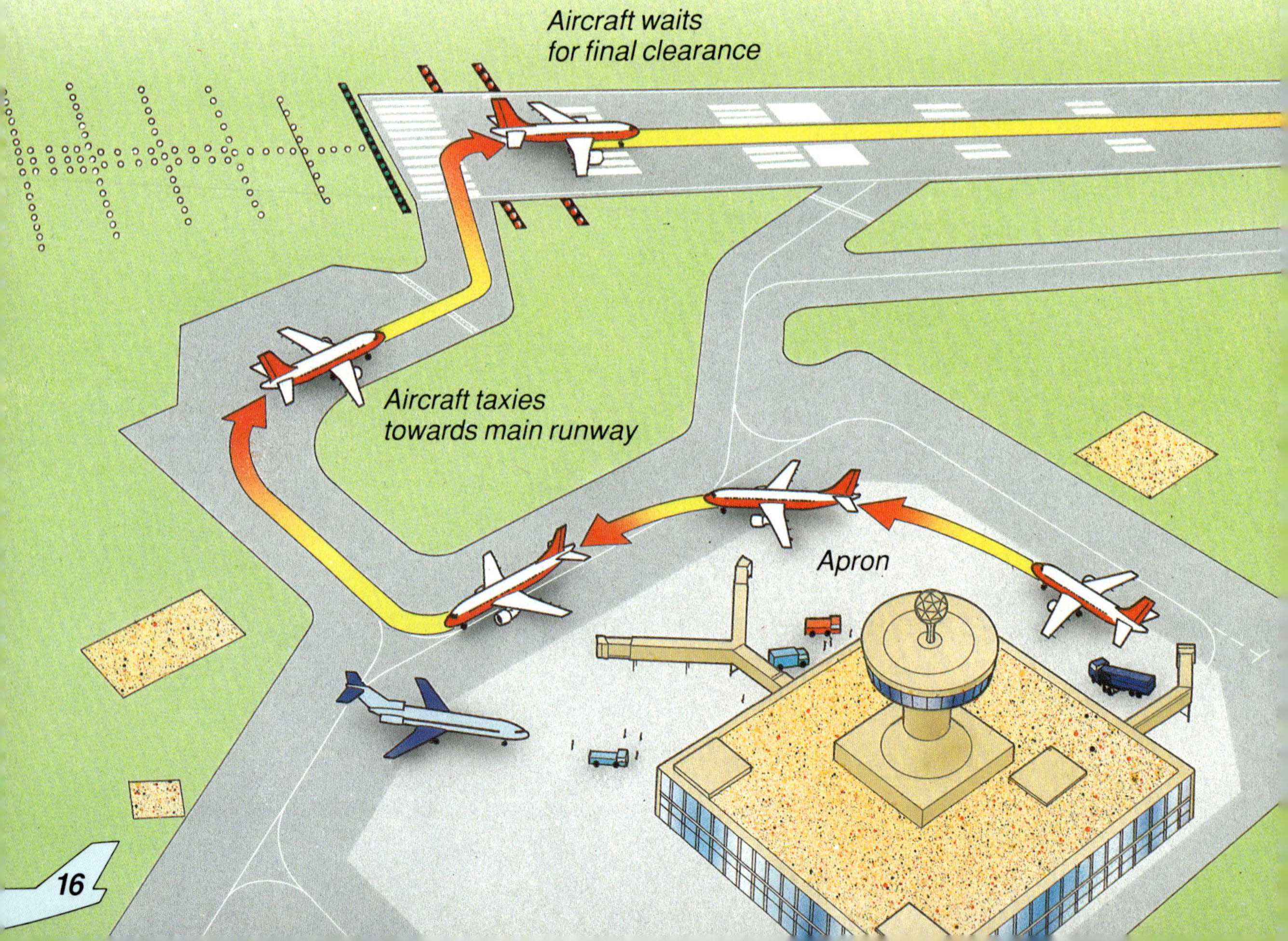

Aircraft waits for final clearance

Aircraft taxies towards main runway

Apron

△ The control tower is the nerve centre of the airport. All aircraft, both in the air and on the ground, are directed under the watchful eyes of staff in the tower.

RADIO TALK

Pilots and air traffic controllers talk to each other over the radio. Sometimes reception is not clear, so to avoid confusion, planes can be identified by using their registration letters. To avoid any confusion, the phonetic or sound alphabet is used, so instead of just saying 'TD', it's 'Tango Delta', which leaves no chance of a misunderstanding.

A	Alfa	N	November
B	Bravo	O	Oscar
C	Charlie	P	Papa
D	Delta	Q	Quebec
E	Echo	R	Romeo
F	Foxtrot	S	Sierra
G	Golf	T	Tango
H	Hotel	U	Uniform
I	India	V	Victor
J	Juliet	W	Whisky
K	Kilo	X	X-ray
L	Lima	Y	Yankee
M	Mike	Z	Zulu

Takeoff

in runway

From parking bay to runway

A typical takeoff sequence goes like this: first the pilot asks the control tower for permission to leave the apron. When this is received engines are started and a small tractor may push the plane back from its parking bay. All the passengers should have their seat belts on by now and the no smoking signs are on in the cabin. The aircraft taxies slowly towards the main runway, under directions from the tower. Here only one runway is shown, but large airports may have two or three. The pilot waits to move onto the runway – an aircraft may be landing, so the tower has to check all's clear first. Then the aircraft can move into position for takeoff. The engines are run up to full thrust, and with a mighty roar, the aircraft accelerates down the runway.

The length of a takeoff run varies from plane to plane. It depends also on the load carried and the weather – wings and engines are less efficient on hot days than on cold ones. A typical run for a fully-loaded Boeing 747 is about 45 seconds. Check your own takeoff against this standard time.

17

INTO THE AIR

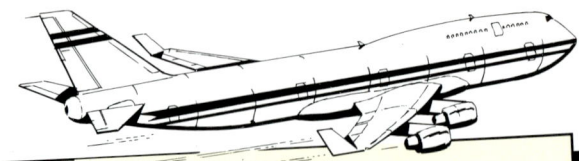

☐ As flying speed is reached, the pilot pulls gently back on the control column. The plane 'rotates', lifting its nose towards the sky. A moment later, the rumble of the wheels stops, the ground falls away and the plane heads towards its cruising height, some 10 km (6.2 miles) above the ground.

But how does it all work? After all, aircraft wings don't flap like those of a bird. The secret lies in the curving wing shape and the high speed air flowing past. All lifting surfaces, called aerofoils, use the fact that fast-moving air rushing across the curved upper surface becomes 'stretched out', giving it a lower pressure. This vacuum effect lifts the wing into the air by suction from above and push from below.

DID YOU KNOW?

✓ Fully loaded with fuel, passengers and cargo, a Boeing 747 weighs about 370 tonnes at takeoff.

✓ Flight crews have two 'decision points' during a takeoff run. V1 is the 'no turning back' point – if nothing has gone wrong up to that moment, the captain commits to a takeoff. V2 is when safety speed has been reached and the plane is climbing away. Normally 'gear up' follows this, and the undercarriage is retracted.

✓ The first Airbus A300 was sent to the scrapyard in 1990 after 16 years of service. In that time it had carried 3,736,550 passengers and made 14,945 flights.

✓ At many airports, the first steep moments of takeoff are followed by a flatter, less powerful ascent. This is to reduce engine power over noise-sensitive places, especially at night.

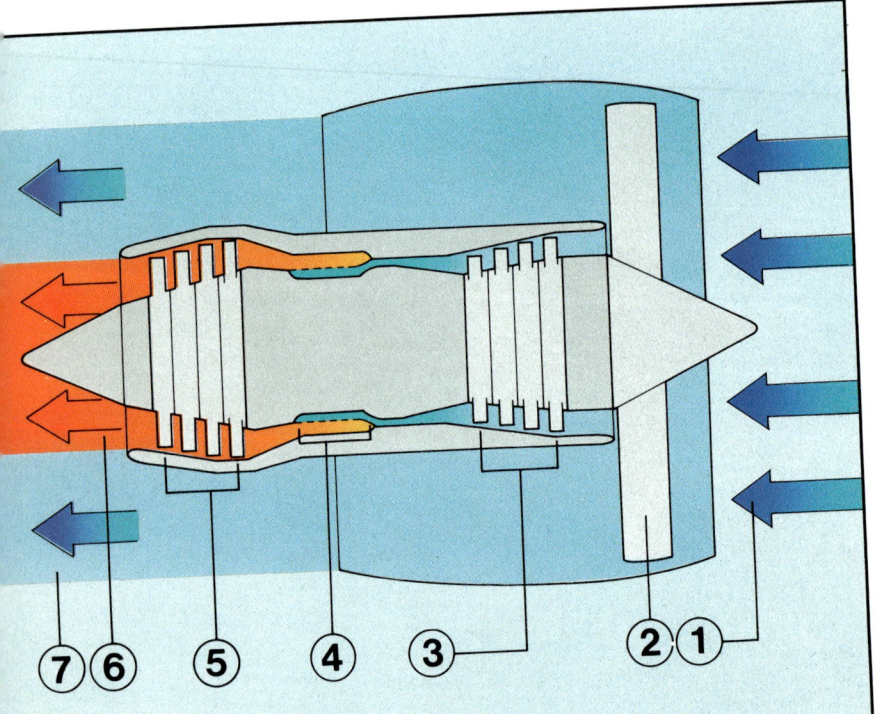

◁ Airliners mostly use turbofan engines for power. Large or small these engines all work in a similar way.
1 Air flows into intake.
2 Front fan sucks in the air.
3 The compressor squashes the air as tightly as possible before it enters the combustion chamber.
4 Fuel is sprayed into the chamber, mixed with the air and ignited. It burns with the air's oxygen, producing hot gases.
5 Hot gases roar through the rear turbine, making it spin, so driving the blades of the front fan and compressor.
6 Hot gases produce thrust.
7 Cold air from the front fan also produce thrust.

Principles of Flight

All aircraft fly through a balance of four forces. **Thrust** from the engines pushes a plane forward, overcoming **drag** caused by air resistance. When the aircraft is moving fast enough, **lift** from the wings overcomes the plane's **weight**, and it takes off.

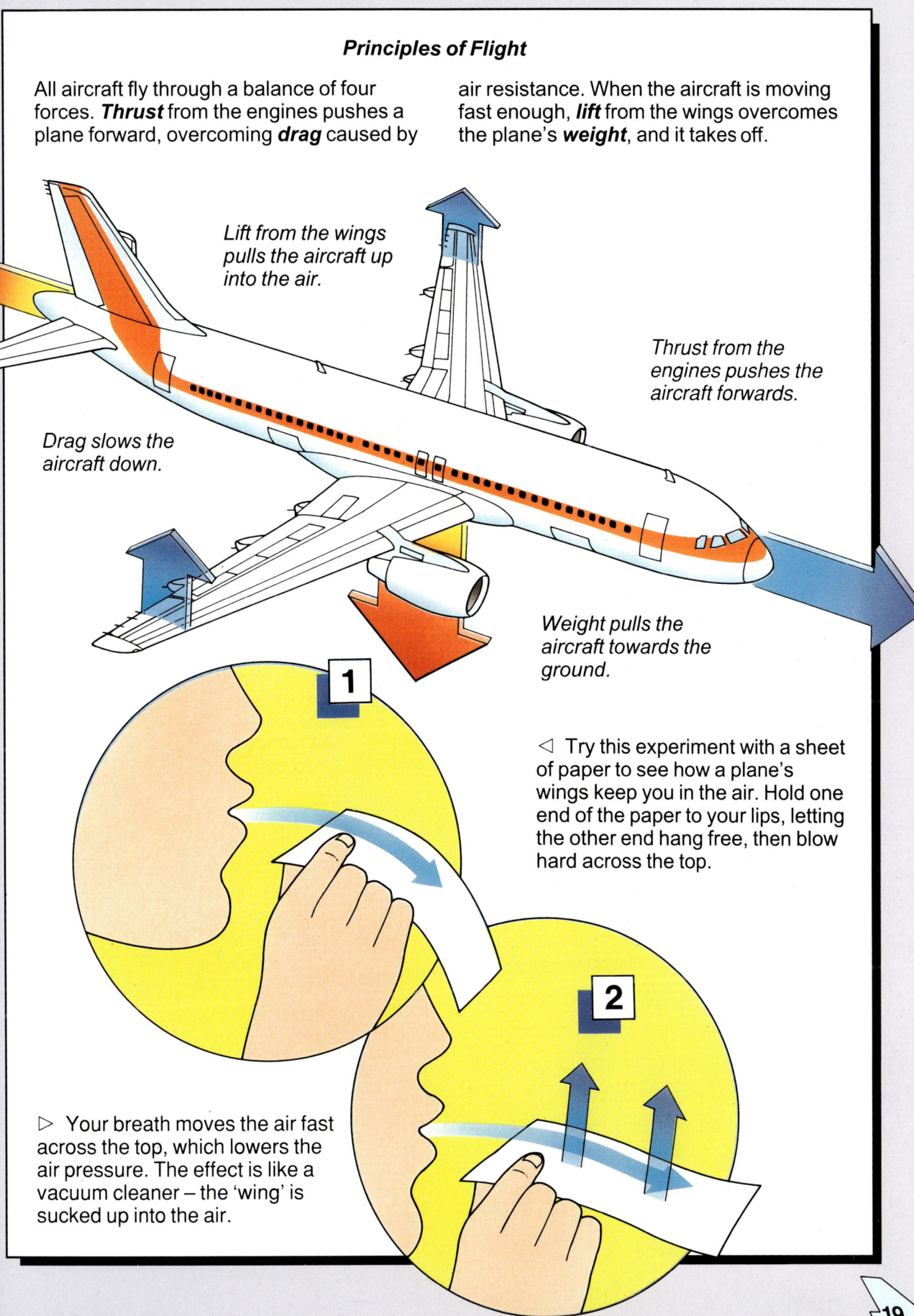

Lift from the wings pulls the aircraft up into the air.

Thrust from the engines pushes the aircraft forwards.

Drag slows the aircraft down.

Weight pulls the aircraft towards the ground.

◁ Try this experiment with a sheet of paper to see how a plane's wings keep you in the air. Hold one end of the paper to your lips, letting the other end hang free, then blow hard across the top.

▷ Your breath moves the air fast across the top, which lowers the air pressure. The effect is like a vacuum cleaner – the 'wing' is sucked up into the air.

19

ABOVE THE CLOUDS

Altitude diagram (km):
- 20 km (12.4 miles) altitude
- 18 — Aerospatiale Concorde
- 16 — Cessna Citation III
- Ozone layer 15–28 km height
- 14 — Canadair Challenger
- Cirrus 'mare's tail' cloud
- 12 — Cirrocumulus 'mackerel' cloud
- 10 — Fokker F100
- Boeing 747
- Boeing 757
- 8
- 6 — Cumulonimbus thunderstorm cloud — Vickers Viscount
- Saab SF340
- 4 — Shorts 360
- 2 — Cumulus puffy fair weather cloud
- Stratus grey rain cloud

Concorde and business jets | Jetliners | Propeller planes

❏ As your jet climbs away from the airport, it usually has to fly through bumpy layers of cloud before reaching the smooth, mostly cloud-free air of the upper atmosphere. It wasn't until the 1950s, when the first jetliners were developed, that the airlines could take their passengers above most of the weather. After the concentration needed during takeoff, the flight crew relax, leaving the computerized automatic pilot to fly the plane. Outside, the sky is clear blue, but thunderstorms can still be a problem, and clear air turbulence, CAT for short, sometimes makes it feel as if the plane is flying on cobblestones. If the ride is going to be rough, the captain will usually order seat belts to be fastened as a precaution.

△ Propeller planes fly at lower altitudes than jetliners, which cruise above most of the weather. The highest flyers of all are small business jets and Concorde.

DID YOU KNOW?

✓ The higher a plane flies, the colder the air around it. At cruising height, the temperature outside your cabin window is about -57°C (-70°F), far colder than the chilliest refrigerator.

✓ Air pressure falls with height too; you would survive only moments outside at cruise height before passing out. To make cabins comfortable, they are pressurized to provide breathing conditions similar to those at much lower heights.

✓ In a typical airliner, cabin air is changed every three minutes or so to keep it fresh and get rid of smells.

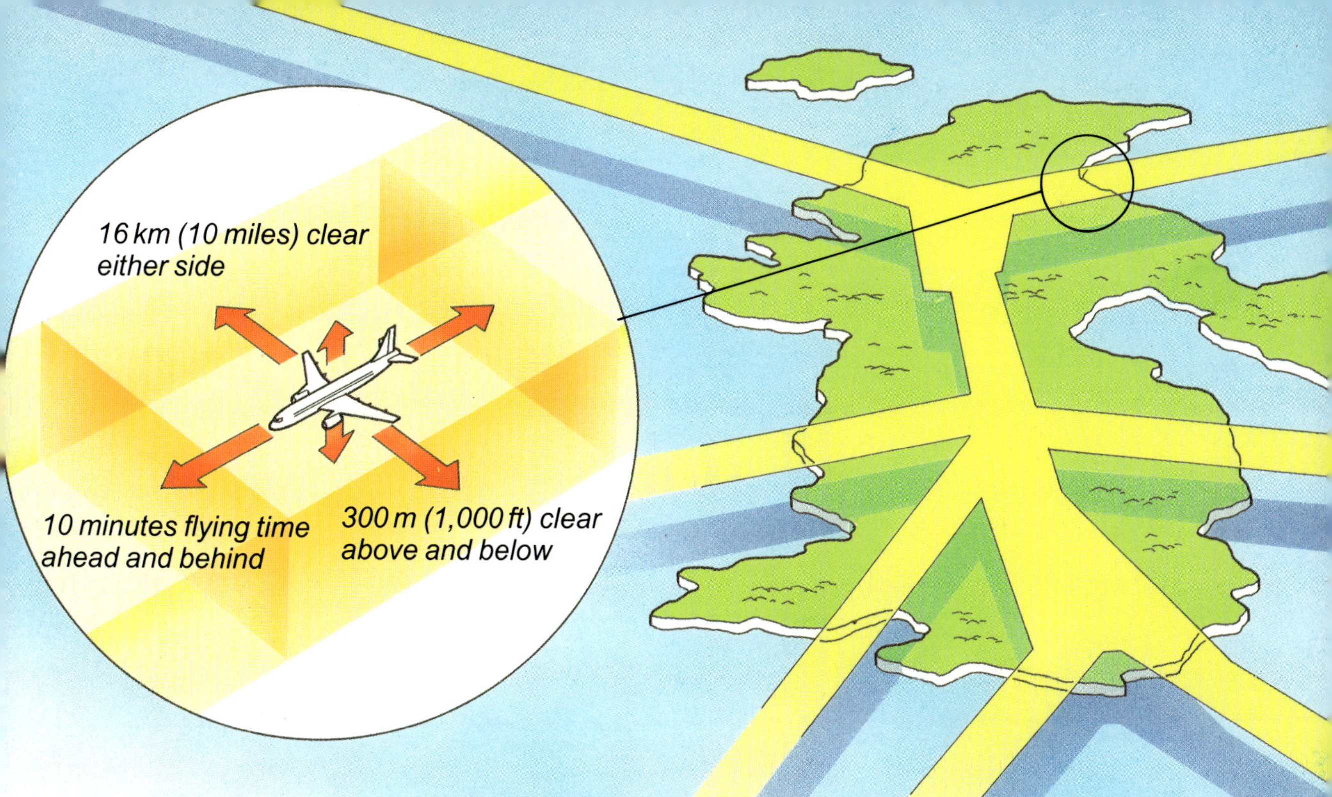

16 km (10 miles) clear either side

10 minutes flying time ahead and behind

300 m (1,000 ft) clear above and below

△ Airliners fly along routes called air lanes. These are like invisible corridors in the sky, with strict rules to separate aircraft inside them. The map shows air corridors, crisscrossing the land below. A pilot keeps on course by flying from radio beacon to radio beacon, using navigation equipment to stay in the air lane.

▷ Radar enables flight crews to keep a check on the weather ahead, and so if necessary avoid thunderstorms. Radar (short for *ra*dio *d*etection *a*nd *r*anging) works by sending out radio signals from a dish-shaped antenna in the aircraft's nose. The radio waves bounce off any reasonably solid object (such as the water droplets in cloud) and return as 'echoes' to be received on the same dish antenna. The echoes are displayed on a small televison screen in the cockpit.

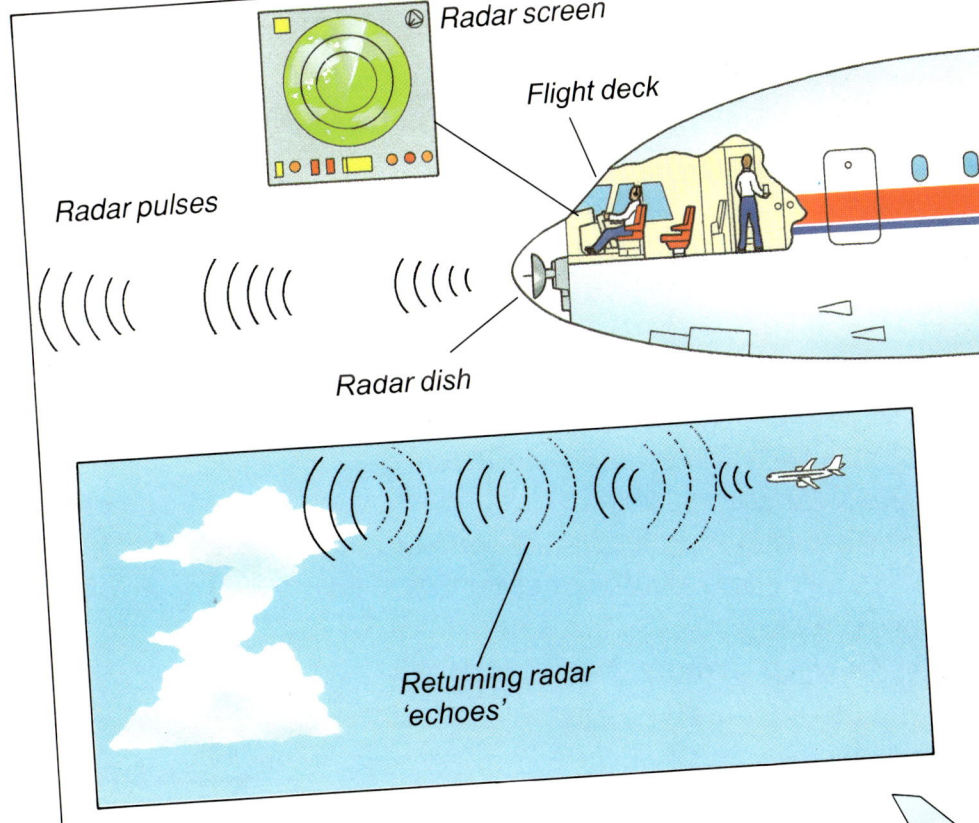

Radar screen

Flight deck

Radar pulses

Radar dish

Returning radar 'echoes'

21

IN FLIGHT

❏ The first thing most people want on a flight after they release their seat belts is a drink and a meal. Food is prepared on the ground and packed into trays. In the galley, cabin staff heat up food in special ovens while drinks orders are being seen to. Then meal trays are passed out to passengers. Apart from the meal, each tray comes with an individually-wrapped set of cutlery, salt and pepper packs, and often a toothpick. Drinks such as tea, coffee and fruit juices are also provided.

Most offer a choice of food, even in economy class. Most main course meals include meat, usually chicken or beef, so vegetarians or those on special diets should order meals when they buy their tickets.

△ Cabin crew heat up food in an aircraft galley. In case of food poisoning, captain and co-pilot are given different meals. This means someone will be fit to fly at all times.

FOOD FACTS

✓ In-flight catering is big business. The annual food shopping list for bigger airlines can include 120,000 tonnes of meat, 3 million litres (658,000 gals) of milk, and 30 tonnes of smoked salmon.

✓ Cabin air can dry you out, so drink plenty of liquid on a long flight.

✓ You lose some of your sense of taste at high altitude. Airline chefs have to take this into account when preparing food and drink.

Individual menus are all part of the service with many airlines.

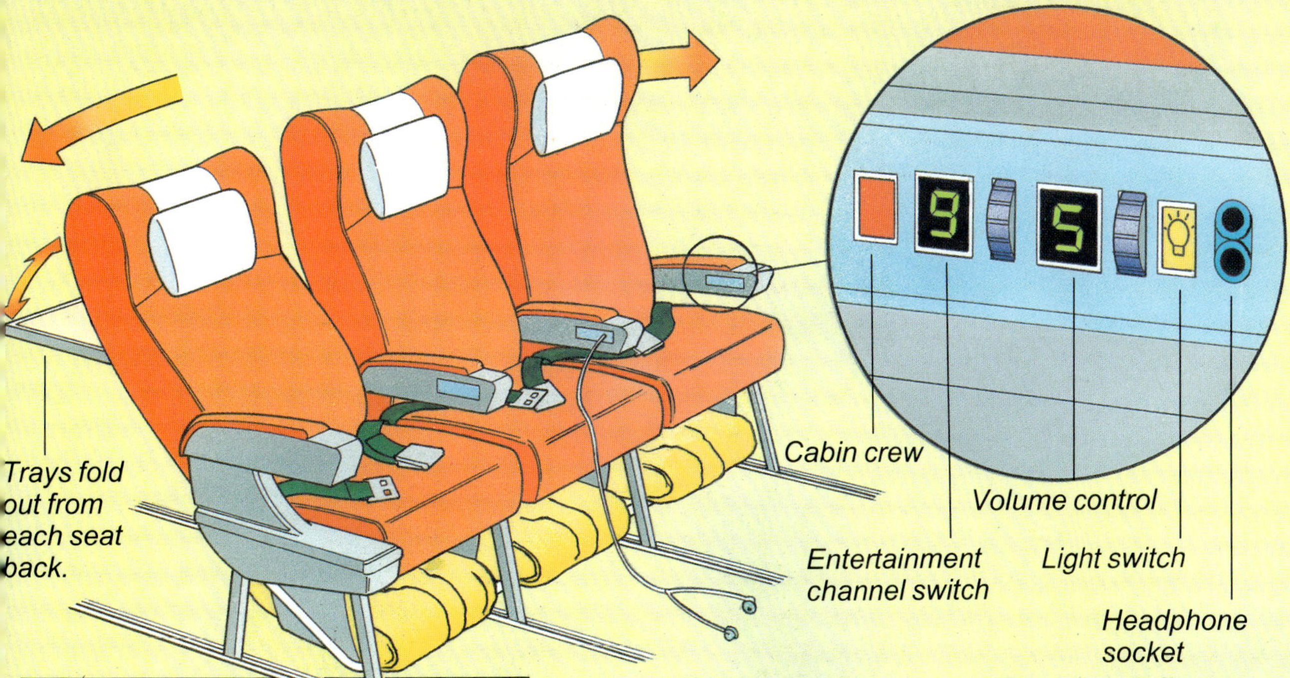

Trays fold out from each seat back.

Cabin crew
Volume control
Entertainment channel switch
Light switch
Headphone socket

△ Seat backs should be upright and belts fastened for takeoff and landing. The seat can be reclined during the flight, but it's a good idea to keep belts fastened loosely. Overhead units contain lights and air vents.

△ These controls are in the arm rests. Headphones are handed out by cabin staff, they provide the sound for up to a dozen channels and for the in-flight movie. This is usually projected onto a screen in each cabin.

Just in case...

In-flight problems are rare, but all airliners have emergency equipment. In case of cabin pressure failure, oxygen masks drop down automatically from positions below the overhead baggage racks. Life rafts are carried in case of a set down on the sea. Cabin crew give instructions for the use of these and the life jackets stored under the seats before every flight. Emergency exits are fitted with inflatable rubber chutes, and to pass safety tests, the aircraft must be capable of being evacuated in 90 seconds or less.

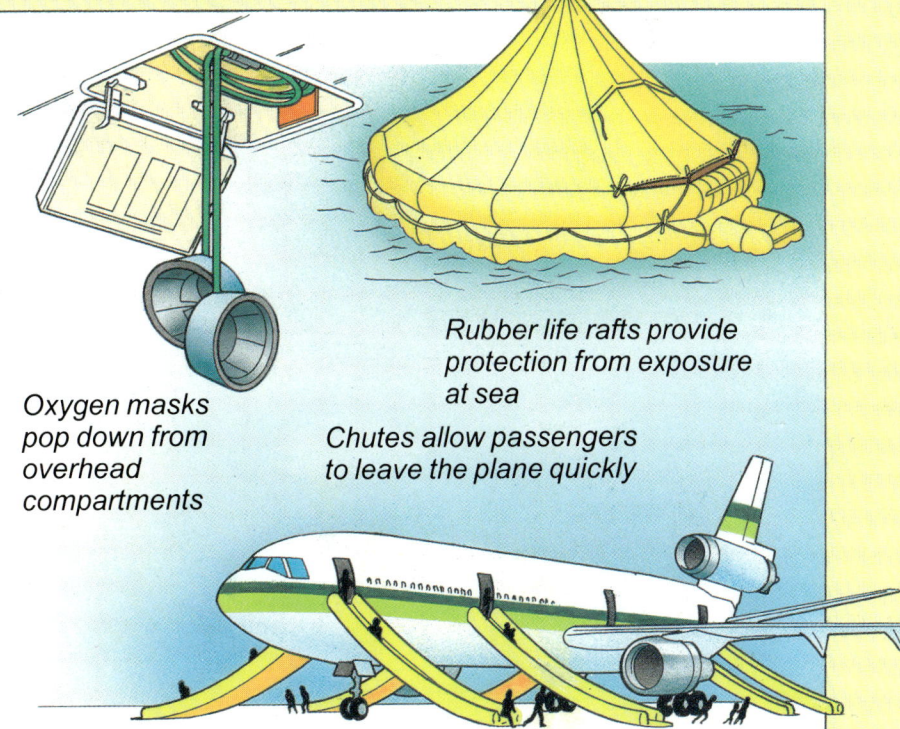

Oxygen masks pop down from overhead compartments

Rubber life rafts provide protection from exposure at sea

Chutes allow passengers to leave the plane quickly

23

ENJOYING THE VIEW

❏ Once a plane is at cruising height, passengers can settle down for the journey. On short trips, such as the flight from London to Paris, the cruise may be no more than a few minutes before the plane noses down for descent. Over long distances though, many hours may pass – flights from Europe to North America, for example, take seven hours or more. Even so, there's little need to get bored, as during daylight hours, there is plenty to look at out of the windows. Most frequently of course, the land below is obscured by the clouds which form in the lower layers of the atmosphere. But through gaps you can usually spot mountains, rivers and coastlines. Flying over polar lands, you can see snow-capped peaks and icy glaciers. Some countries are spectacular from the air. The Atlantic island of Iceland, for example, is covered in volcanic cones, and seeing them from the air is better than any geography lesson.

Taking photographs

Taking photos through cabin windows is not difficult providing you follow some simple rules. Don't let the sun shine directly into the lens to avoid glare. Support the camera firmly to prevent blurred pictures. Get some foreground interest into the shot, such as a section of wing. If you have a video camera, hold it firmly to avoid picture shake. The microphone will pick up cabin and engine noise, but a commentary will give viewers something interesting to listen to. Video shots are especially interesting on takeoff, turns near cloud formations and on landing. Here again, you need to prop the camera firmly against your shoulder to prevent too much of a lurch when the plane's wheels hit the runway.

△ For a grandstand view of the world below, get a window seat. You usually have to shut the sliding blind when an in-flight movie is showing.

△ Once the plane is above the clouds, you get a 'plan view' of the weather from above. Take a weather book and try spotting different cloud formations.

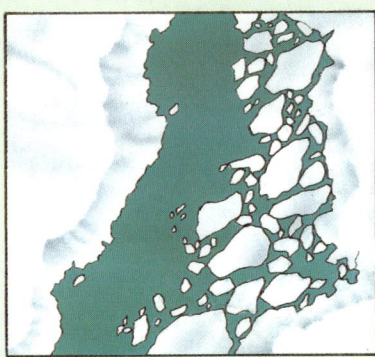

△ Flying can be an aerial geography lesson. Iceland's volcanoes are spectacular from the air, as is the pack ice of Hudson's Bay in Canada, shown above.

△ Wings flex up and down slightly during flight. Don't worry though – they are meant to! Without some give in the wing structure, they would snap off in gusts.

△ On flights over the Alps, pilots sometimes bank the aircraft to give passengers a good view of such sights as Mont Blanc, Europe's highest mountain peak.

△ The captain usually gives flight details on the intercom. Some planes have cabin signs showing height and speed.

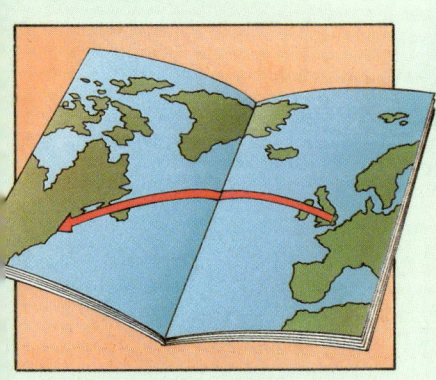

△ To track your flight's progress, take an atlas with you. It will be much better than the small-scale maps printed in the airline magazines carried aboard.

△ Flying west, jets are 'chasing the sun', resulting in long, beautiful sunsets. Flying east, dawn comes up very quickly as the plane flies towards the sun.

△ Night flights allow you to spot city lights down below. From cruising height, you can see brightly lit highways too, though car lights are impossible to make out.

APPROACH AND LANDING

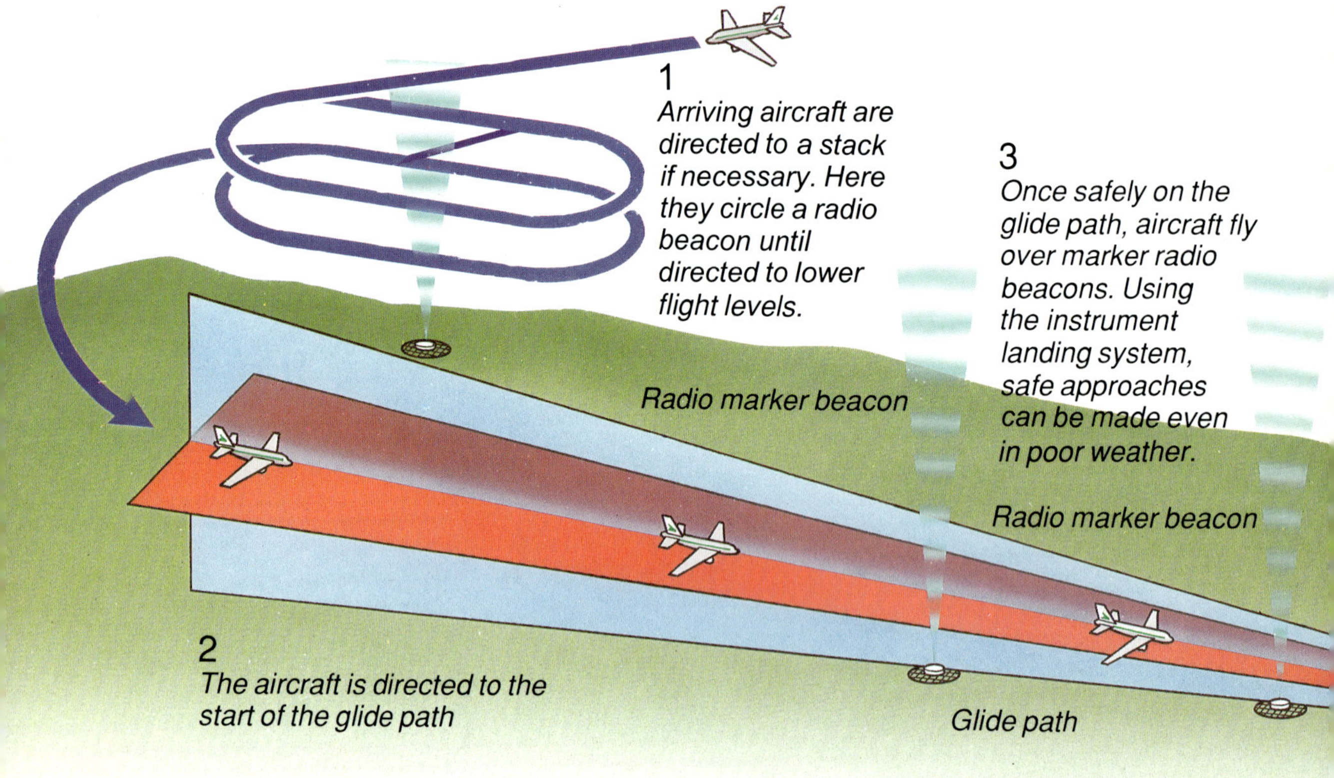

1 Arriving aircraft are directed to a stack if necessary. Here they circle a radio beacon until directed to lower flight levels.

3 Once safely on the glide path, aircraft fly over marker radio beacons. Using the instrument landing system, safe approaches can be made even in poor weather.

Radio marker beacon

Radio marker beacon

2 The aircraft is directed to the start of the glide path

Glide path

❏ As a flight nears its end, the pilot contacts approach control at the destination airport, asking for permission to land.

Approach controllers are responsible for aircraft arriving from different directions. Only one can land at a time, so if several arrive together they are ordered to fly in a 'stack', a number of circling planes, slowly descending in turn until it is their turn to land. Once at the bottom of the stack, a plane is directed onto the glide path, a straight line approach to the runway.

The glide path is formed by two radio beams from the airport, forming an invisible cross-shaped slope in the sky. Cockpit instruments show when the aircraft is on the right course.

△ As the aircraft slows for landing, the flaps are lowered. These are rear sections of the wings, which slow the plane down. Lowered flaps increase buffeting a little, but this is normal.

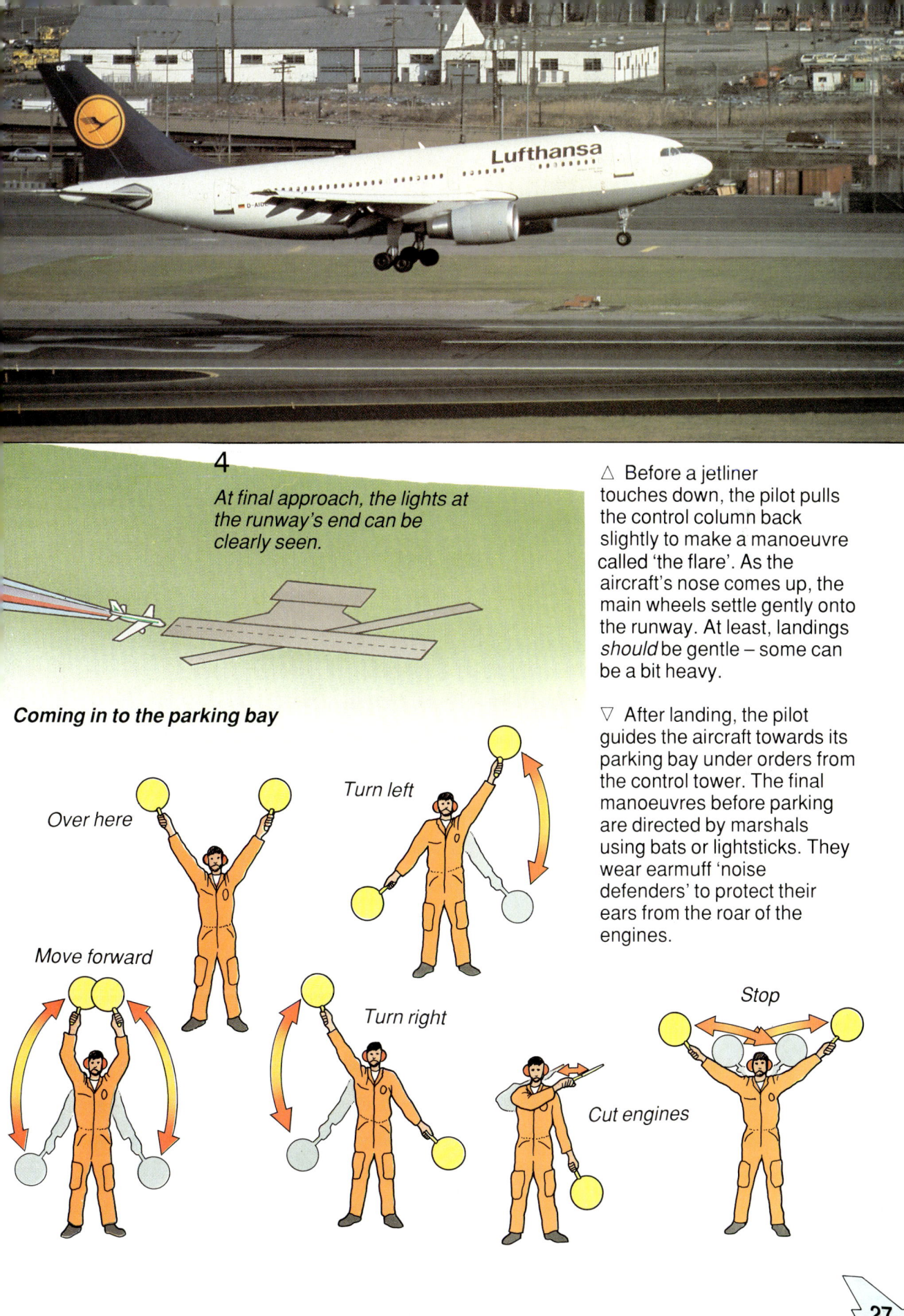

4

At final approach, the lights at the runway's end can be clearly seen.

△ Before a jetliner touches down, the pilot pulls the control column back slightly to make a manoeuvre called 'the flare'. As the aircraft's nose comes up, the main wheels settle gently onto the runway. At least, landings *should* be gentle – some can be a bit heavy.

Coming in to the parking bay

▽ After landing, the pilot guides the aircraft towards its parking bay under orders from the control tower. The final manoeuvres before parking are directed by marshals using bats or lightsticks. They wear earmuff 'noise defenders' to protect their ears from the roar of the engines.

Over here

Turn left

Move forward

Turn right

Cut engines

Stop

AIRPORT SAFETY

❏ Millions of people travel by air every year, and flying is one of the safest ways to travel, but emergencies do happen. So airports have to maintain fully equipped fire-fighting, rescue and medical services, ready for action at a moment's notice.

Major airports have several types of fire trucks. These range from small and fast RIVs (Rapid Intervention Vehicles) to big heavy-duty crash tenders. All are equipped with foam sprays to smother flames, water supplies, medical equipment and rescue tools to cut into an aircraft fuselage if necessary.

Airport safety includes a lot more than just emergency cover. Runways have to be kept clear of snow and ice, lighting, radio and radar systems have to be maintained in perfect order. Even bird scarers are important, to keep flocks of birds away from runway approaches.

△ This Rapid Intervention Vehicle can speed along at 112 km/h (70 mph).

▽ Keeping runways clear of snow is a job carried out by snowplough trucks.

▷ Heavy-duty crash tenders are equipped with foam monitors to spray on flames. This one also mounts a telescopic platform to fight fires from above.

▷ Aircraft wings lose much of their lifting power if they get coated with ice. In very cold weather, spray equipment is used to drench wings in de-icer fluid.

◁ Emergency crews practise regularly, often setting fire to old aircraft fuselages for realism. Here a fire-fighting team uses foam spray equipment to quench flames in a few minutes.

Bird strikes and black boxes

Birds are a danger to low-flying aircraft. Engines can be damaged and windscreens smashed if a plane flies into a flock of birds. The windscreen shown here (from a Boeing 747) has multiple layers, partly for strength to resist a bird strike and partly to provide electric layers for demisting and heating at high altitude. Keeping birds away from airports can be a problem, especially for airports on migration routes. Models of birds of prey can be used as scarecrows. Other remedies include loud sirens, firework explosions or simply chasing the birds away.

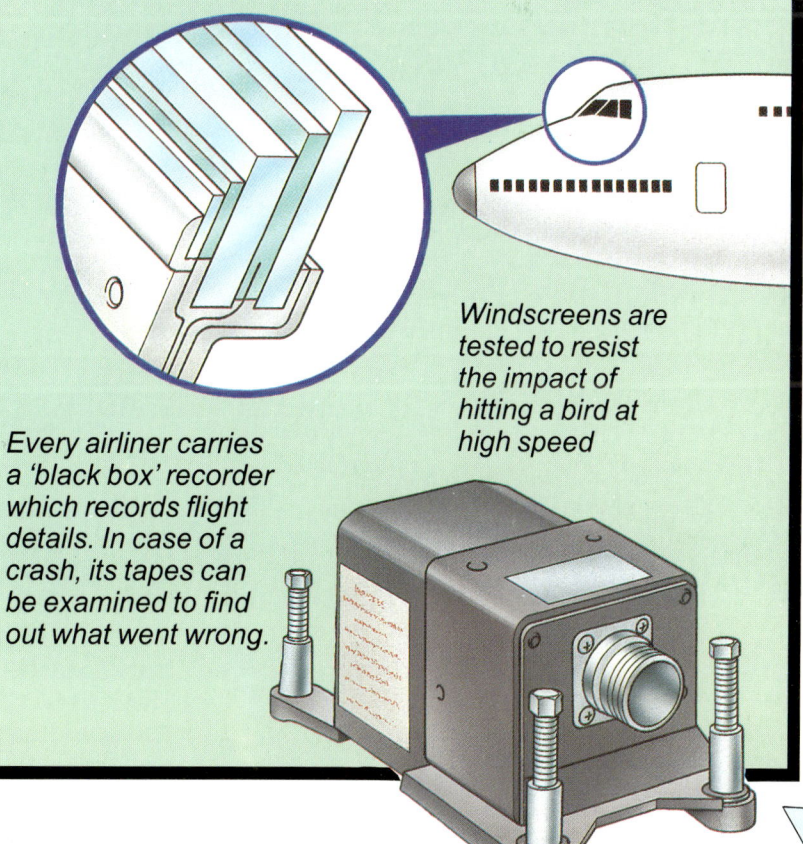

Windscreens are tested to resist the impact of hitting a bird at high speed

Every airliner carries a 'black box' recorder which records flight details. In case of a crash, its tapes can be examined to find out what went wrong.

29

PLANE SPOTTING

❏ At first glance most jetliners look so similar that it seems impossible to tell them apart. Different markings help of course, but the art of telling an A300 from an A310 is something you only pick up with practice. Look out for the small differences which act as spotting clues – here, for example, the shorter nose of the A310 gives it away as a smaller version of its big sister.

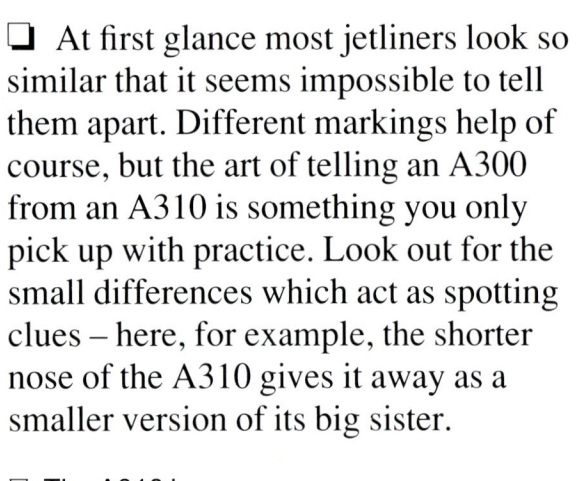

▽ The American twinjet Boeing 737 is very popular for short and medium distance routes.

▽ The Airbus A300 is built by a group of European manufacturers.

▽ The A310 is a smaller version of the A300, designed for short routes.

◁ The twin-engined Boeing 737 is the world's most popular jetliner. By December 1990, over 2,400 had been ordered by world airlines.

△ The A320 is the world's first airliner with all its systems controlled by computers. The pilots fly the aircraft using side-stick controls.

Registration marks

All airliners have registration letters, which act as identifying codes, much like the number plate on your family car. Every country has its own letter code. Here are some of the most common ones.

Australia	VH	India	VT
Austria	OE	Italy	I
Belgium	OO	Japan	JA
Brazil	PP or PT	Malaysia	9M
Canada	C	Netherlands	PH
China	B	Saudi Arabia	HZ
Denmark	OY	USSR	CCCP
Egypt	SU	Spain	EC
Eire	EI, EJ	Switzerland	HB
France	F	Turkey	TC
Germany	D	United Kingdom	G
Greece	SX	USA	N
Hong Kong	VR-H	Zambia	9J

△ In which country is this airliner registered?

◁ Boeing's 767 competes with the A300 for medium haul business.

▽ The McDonnell-Douglas MD-80 is another popular twinjet, with over 1,100 sold.

△ The short-range Dutch Fokker F100 is popular both in Europe and the USA.

▷ The slim-fuselage Boeing 757 has been christened the 'stick insect' by keen aircraft spotters!

31

Plane spotting 2 / The big jets

◁ One of the first three-jet designs, 1,821 Boeing 727s were made from 1963 to 1984.

▽ Lockheed's TriStar flies long range routes.

▽ The McDonnell Douglas MD-11 has wingtip fins and high-mounted tail engine.

Sack the signwriter!

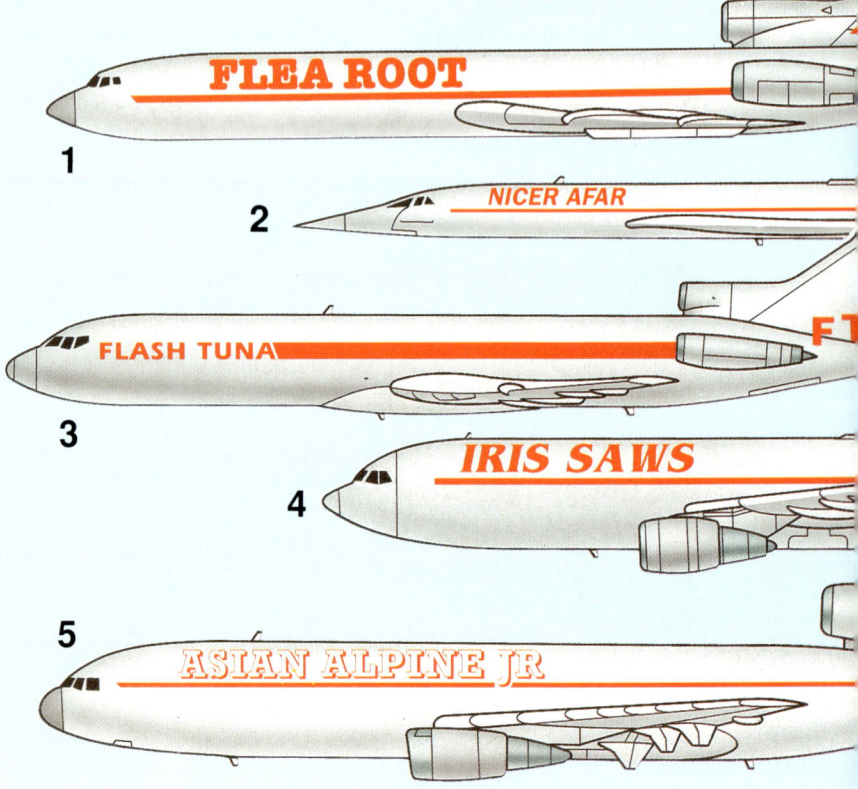

Someone has played a joke at the airlines' expense and repainted the airline names. Now no one can see which plane is theirs. See if you can unscramble the letters to make the names of six world airlines. The answers are on page 40.

Painting an aircraft is not just for advertising the airline name. Correctly applied, paint helps protect the metal underneath from scratches and corrosion, which can weaken the structure. Lots of paint is used. Over 100 litres (22 gals) of top coat is needed to cover a medium-sized jet.

32

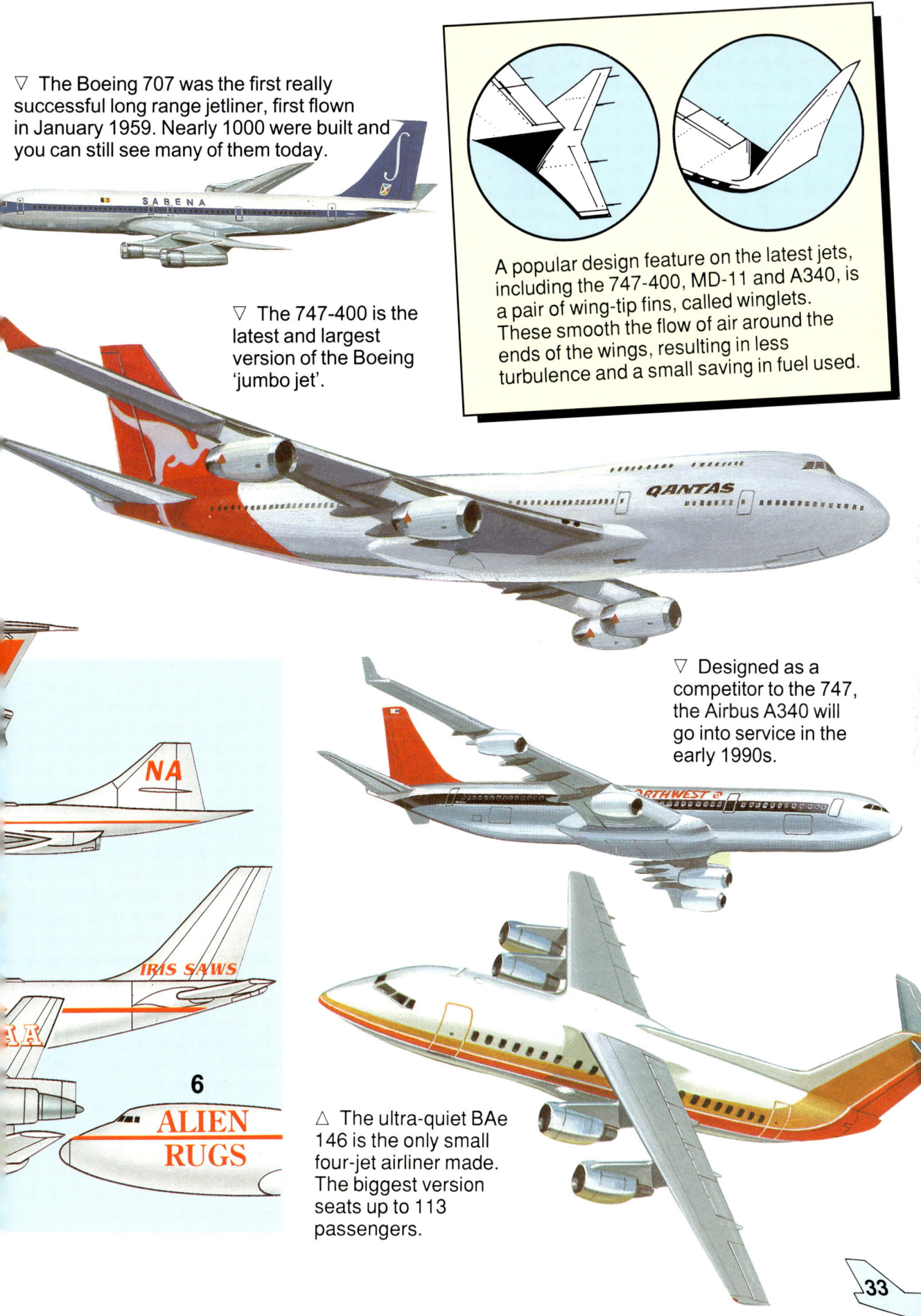

▽ The Boeing 707 was the first really successful long range jetliner, first flown in January 1959. Nearly 1000 were built and you can still see many of them today.

▽ The 747-400 is the latest and largest version of the Boeing 'jumbo jet'.

A popular design feature on the latest jets, including the 747-400, MD-11 and A340, is a pair of wing-tip fins, called winglets. These smooth the flow of air around the ends of the wings, resulting in less turbulence and a small saving in fuel used.

▽ Designed as a competitor to the 747, the Airbus A340 will go into service in the early 1990s.

△ The ultra-quiet BAe 146 is the only small four-jet airliner made. The biggest version seats up to 113 passengers.

TIME ZONES

❏ One problem with which both passengers and flight crews have to cope is jet lag, caused by covering long distances on east-west flights. These journeys cross the 24 time zones, each an hour apart, which divide up the world. Jet lag is the confusion caused by your 'body clock' insisting that it is still lunchtime in London, when you have flown to, say Miami in the USA, where it is still early morning.

There is no real cure for jet lag, other than rest, and gradually getting used to the time at your destination. But you can help your body along by forgetting about time back home, and going on to your destination-zone time immediately you get on board the plane. Adults are often more affected by jet lag than children, so mum and dad may well be a bit grouchy for the first few days abroad! Jet lag is only a real problem on long east-west flights, and no problem at all on journeys going north-south where the entire flight may be in the same zone.

| Time you leave | + | Length of time in the air | +/- | number of time zones you cross |

◁ This diagram shows how to calculate the time when you land. Take away time zone hours for westbound flights, add them for journeys going east. Daylight saving times often throw the sums out though, so always check with a member of the cabin staff.

← Westbound, take away hours   Eastbound, add hours →

INTERNATIONAL TIME ZONES

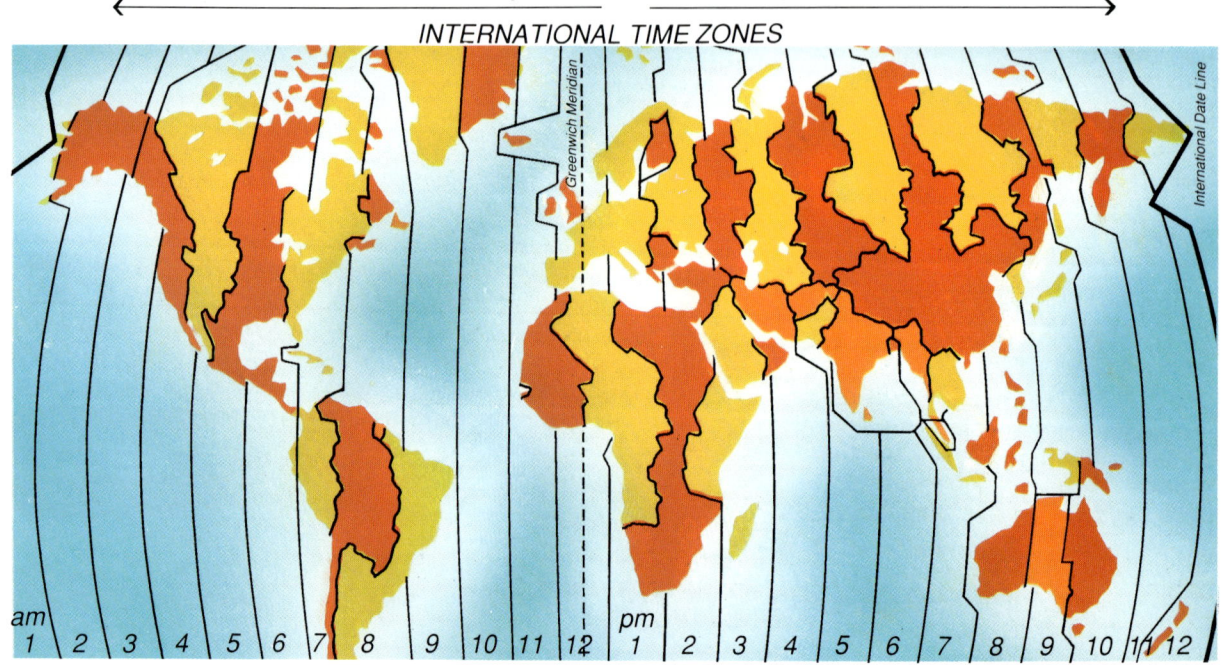

AIR FACTS

Q What is the world's biggest passenger jet?
A At present the Boeing 747-400 holds the title. This aircraft measures almost 71 m (232 ft) long and can carry 412 passengers.

Q When were cabin staff introduced?
A In 1930, by Boeing Air Transport. They were trained as nurses, to care for people who became airsick. Stewardesses also helped clean the planes after flights.

Q What is the world's most successful airliner?
A The Douglas DC-3, of which over 13,000 were built, though this total includes many DC-3s built as troop transports during World War II.

Q When was the 'Golden Age' of flying boats?
A The 1930s, when flying boats were used for almost all long distance flights. Airlines such as Imperial Airways made comfort their watchword and had cabin service and freshly-cooked food rival the best hotels.

Q When did the first jet carry passengers?
A On 2 May, 1952, the British de Havilland Comet I went into service with the airline BOAC.

Q What is a noise footprint?
A It is the ground area under a plane which is affected by the sound of its jet engines. Since the development of the turbofan engine, noise around airports has become less of a problem: fan jets are quieter than the turbojets which propelled early jetliners, and still power Concorde.

Q What is the quietest jetliner?
A The BAe 146 is generally reckoned as the world's quietest. It can fly into some very noise-sensitive airports at night because of this.

Q How are pilots trained?
A By a three-year training course, which teaches them the basics of flying an airliner. Many years of service as co-pilot follow and typically, a pilot becomes captain of a large airliner only after 20–30 years flying experience. Throughout this time, pilots have regular health checks and practise in life-like cockpit simulators, in which emergency situations can be run through and pilots' flying skills checked.

Q What do the crew do before a flight?
A Crews check in about an hour before a flight and study a computer print-out, which covers all the details of the flight: number of passengers and weight of baggage on board, the weather, possible routes and so on. When all has been agreed, the captain signs and accepts the flight plan and the flight dispatch officer files it. Copies are sent by teleprinter to all control points along the route. Carrying all the maps and charts they need, the crew can now go to their aircraft.

△ Stamps issued by various countries to mark the importance of air mail services.

35

THE STORY OF AIRLINERS

❏ The Wright brothers became the world's first aviators when they made the first-ever controlled flights on 17 December 1903. It took another 11 years before the first daily passenger service started. This was a 23 minute run, carrying a single passenger, between two towns in Florida, USA. Since then, with interruptions caused by two world wars, commercial aviation has progressed in leaps and bounds. Today there are over 800 major international airports across the world. In a typical year, London's Heathrow airport alone handles over 40 million passengers and every day the airport has more than 1,000 takeoffs and landings.

△ **1919.** Vickers Vimy Commercial, based on a World War I bomber.

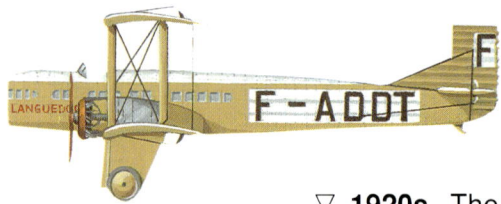

△ **1920s.** Farman Goliath, flew between Paris and London.

◁ **1930s.** Handley Page HP42, flew from Britain to Africa.

▽ **1920s.** The Ford Trimotor, made of ribbed metal, was popular in the USA. It seated 11–14 passengers in wicker seats. Over 200 were built.

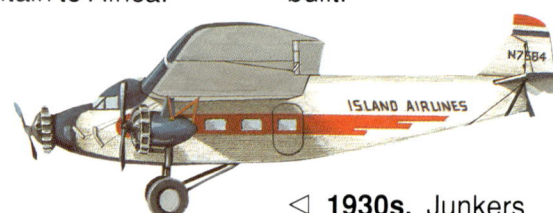

◁ **1930s.** Junkers Ju52. This German three-engine design seated 15–17 passengers.

◁ Flying boats, such as the Short Calcutta, were popular in the 1920s and 1930s for long overwater flights. Engines were unreliable and in an emergency, such aircraft could set down on the ocean.

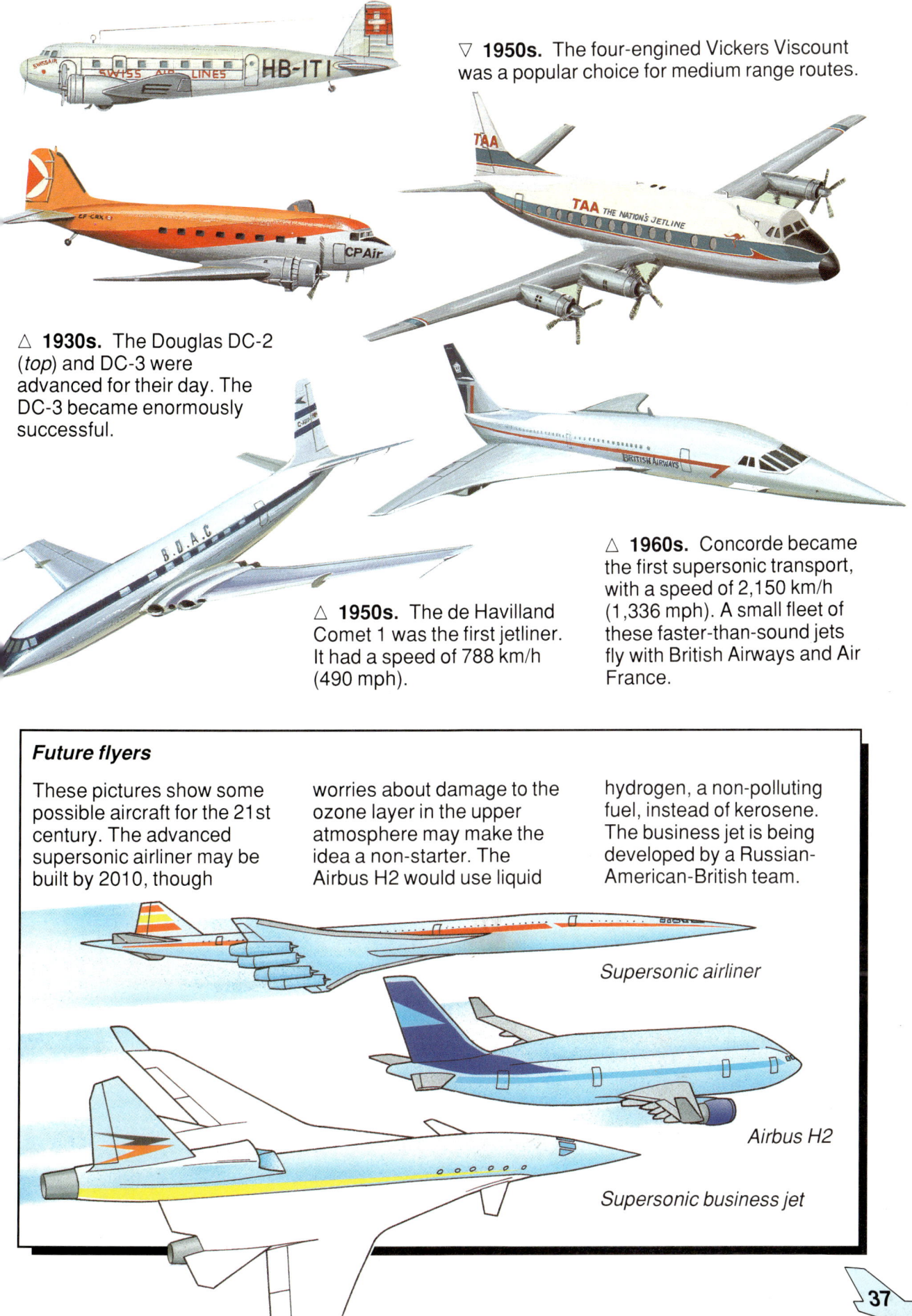

▽ **1950s.** The four-engined Vickers Viscount was a popular choice for medium range routes.

△ **1930s.** The Douglas DC-2 (*top*) and DC-3 were advanced for their day. The DC-3 became enormously successful.

△ **1950s.** The de Havilland Comet 1 was the first jetliner. It had a speed of 788 km/h (490 mph).

△ **1960s.** Concorde became the first supersonic transport, with a speed of 2,150 km/h (1,336 mph). A small fleet of these faster-than-sound jets fly with British Airways and Air France.

Future flyers

These pictures show some possible aircraft for the 21st century. The advanced supersonic airliner may be built by 2010, though worries about damage to the ozone layer in the upper atmosphere may make the idea a non-starter. The Airbus H2 would use liquid hydrogen, a non-polluting fuel, instead of kerosene. The business jet is being developed by a Russian-American-British team.

Supersonic airliner

Airbus H2

Supersonic business jet

GLOSSARY

Aerofoil
Technical term for a lifting surface such as a wing.

Aileron
Small flap-like surface at the rear of each wing. Tilted up and down using the control column to bank an aircraft left and right.

Aircraft movement
Aviation term for a takeoff or landing.

Approach control
Part of the airport control system responsible for guiding aircraft to a safe landing.

Boarding gate
Place where you get on an aircraft, beyond the departure lounge.

Check in
Part of the terminal where you give in your ticket and place your baggage for weighing and loading.

Clear air turbulence
Bumpy air not connected with any visible cloud formation.

Control tower
Nerve centre of an airport, in charge of all aircraft on the ground and in the air.

Departure lounge
Area beyond passport control where you wait to be called to the correct departure gate.

Flaps
Movable surface at the trailing (rear) edge of each wing. Lowered on takeoff and landing to increase lift.

Galley
Kitchen area, used for the preparation of drinks and food.

Glide path
Straight line sloping approach to an airport. Aircraft are guided by radio beacons directly to the end of the runway.

Hydrant tanker
Type of refuelling vehicle that contains a powerful pump but no fuel itself. It joins an underground fuel system to an aircraft's fuel tank.

▽ Every pilot has to file a flight plan before takeoff. It shows the route, height and speed required. Air traffic controllers check the plan and may change it according to weather conditions, or the amount of air traffic already on that route. The strip of paper below is a typical flight plan.
1 Requested starting time.
2 Estimated departure time.
3 Actual departure time.
4 Cruising height.
5 Call sign.
6 Type of aircraft.
7 Speed.
8 Code for destination and route being flown.
9 Radar code.
10 Computer code.
The lower diagram shows how flights are flown in sectors, with fuel used being carefully calculated as the flight progresses. Enough fuel is always carried on an airliner to allow stacking time in the air at the destination, and a diversion to another airport if necessary, due to very bad weather or other difficulty.

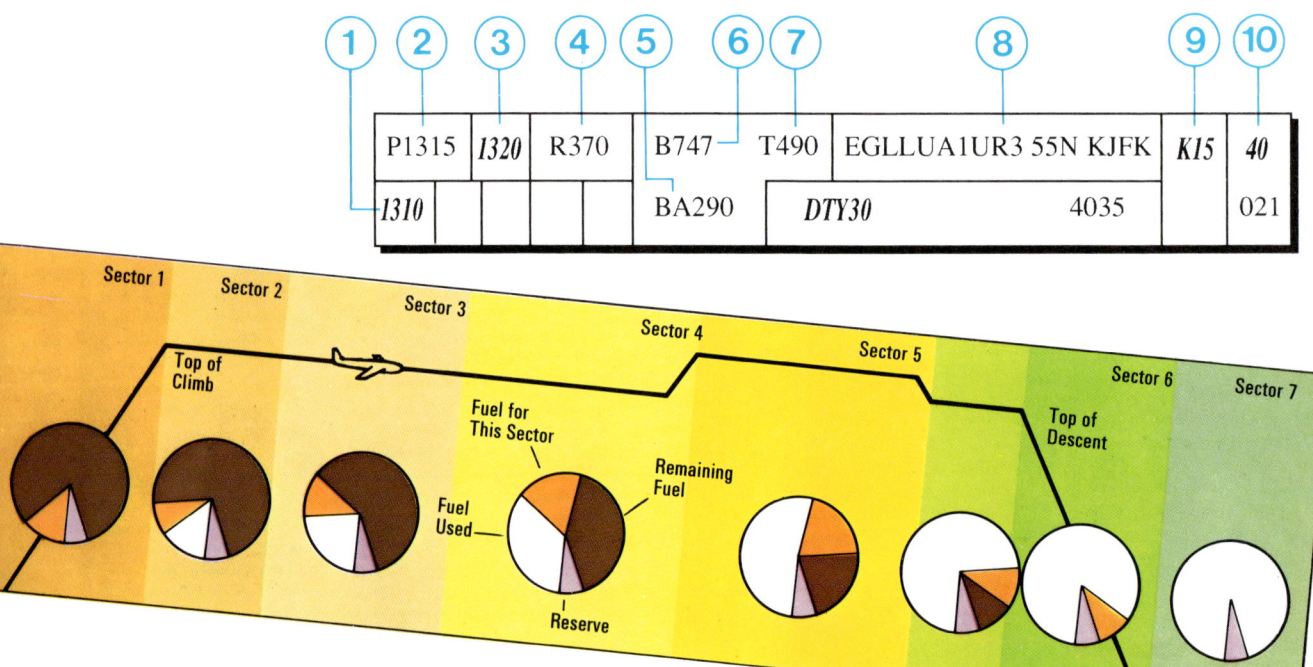

Jet lag
Tiredness and general disorientation caused by your body clock adjusting to the different time in another part of the world. Flight crews 'adjust' mainly by simply sleeping in a regular pattern, even though it may be day at the arrival airport.

Kerosene
Type of petroleum-based fuel used by jet airliners.

Noise footprint
Area of ground affected by jet noise.

Ozone layer
Part of the upper atmosphere which absorbs much of the Sun's ultraviolet rays (those which cause sunburn). Presently there are holes in the ozone layer above parts of the north and south poles. Scientists believe future supersonic airliners may destroy part of the ozone layer, so tests are being carried out to check this.

Passport control
Section of an airport where your passports are checked, both on departure and on arrival.

Radar
Early warning device, used to warn of thunderstorms and other aircraft.

Rapid intervention vehicle
High speed fire-fighting truck, used to deal quickly with an emergency.

Security check
Part of an airport where people are searched. Equipped with X-ray scanners and magnetic detectors, staff carry out hand searches as well, and dogs are often used to sniff out drugs.

Simulator
Life-size copy of an aircraft cockpit. Used for training air crew. Especially useful for practising emergency situations, without any danger to people or aircraft.

△ Inside the control tower at Pearson International Airport, Toronto, Canada.

Stack
Descending group of aircraft, circling a radio beacon while they wait to be given permission to land.

Supersonic
Faster than the speed of sound. At sea level, this is about 1223 km/h (760 mph), falling to 1062 km/h (660 mph) with height. Concorde is currently the only supersonic airliner.

Terminal
Part of an airport which handles the passengers.

Turbofan
Quiet engine used by most airliners. Combines a large front fan with a centrally-mounted jet engine.

Turbojet
Early type of jet engine, much noisier than the later turbofan. It uses more fuel too.

Turnaround
Speedy emptying and refuelling of an airliner between flights.

V1, V2
Decision points during a takeoff. V1 point is the commitment to a takeoff. Before this, there is room to stop on the runway. V2 is when a safe climbing speed is reached.

Vaccination
Medical injection, sometimes needed when visiting a foreign country to prevent you catching diseases there.

Visa
Permission to enter a foreign country. Usually in the form of a stamp in your passport or a separate form.

Winglets
Small fins mounted at the wingtips of some modern airliners, including the 747-400, MD-11 and Airbus A340. They smooth the airflow around the wing and reduce the amount of fuel used.

X-ray
Invisible beam which passes through most solids, but not metals. Used to check inside bags without having to open them. A TV screen displays the bags, and anything metal shows up on the screen.

INDEX

Africa 36
aircraft layout 12, 13
aircraft registration marks 31

aircraft types
Aerospatiale Concorde 13, 16, 20, 36, 37, 39
Airbus
   A300 13, 18, 30
   A310 30
   A320 12, 13, 30
   A340 33, 39
   H2 37
British Aerospace BAe 146 33, 35
Boeing
   707 33
   727 32
   737 30
   747 13, 14, 17, 19, 20, 33, 35, 39
   757 20, 31
   767 25, 31
Canadair Challenger 20
Cessna Citation 20
de Havilland Comet 1 35, 37
Douglas
   DC-2, DC-3 35, 37
   DC-7C 37
Farman Goliath 36
Fokker F100 20, 31
Ford Trimotor 36
Handley Page HP42 36
Junkers Ju 52 36
Lockheed TriStar 32
McDonnell-Douglas
   MD-11 32, 33, 39
   MD-80 13, 31
Saab SF340 20
Short Calcutta 36
Shorts 360
Vickers
   Vimy 36
   Viscount 20

air lanes 21

airlines
Air France 37
BOAC 35
Boeing Air Transport 35
Britannia Airways 25
British Airways 37
Imperial Airways 35

air mail 35

airports
Doha 4
Heathrow 4, 7, 36
Kennedy 6
Montreal 11
O'Hare 4
Pearson 39

air traffic control 4, 16, 17
Alps 25
approach control 26, 38
Atlantic Ocean 24

bird strikes 29
black box recorder 29
boarding gate 9, 38
Britain 36
business jets 20, 37

Canada 11, 25
check-in 8, 38
clear air turbulence 20, 38
cloud formations 20, 21, 25
control tower 16, 17, 38

departure lounge 9, 38

emergency equipment 23
Europe 4, 24, 25

flight controls 14, 15
flight instruments 14, 15
flight plan 35, 38
Florida 36
flying boats 35, 36
future aircraft types 37

glide path 26, 38

Hudson's Bay 25

Iceland 24, 25
in-flight catering 22

jetlag 34, 39
jetliners 20

landing 26, 27
lift 18, 19
London 24, 34, 36

metal detector 9
Miami 34
Mont Blanc 25

New York 6
noise footprint 35, 39
North America 24

ozone layer 20, 37, 39

painting aircraft 32
Paris 24, 36
parking marshals 27
passenger flow 7
passports 9, 39
Persian Gulf 4
photography 24
principles of flight 18, 19
propeller planes 20

radar 16, 21, 39
rapid intervention vehicle 28, 39
refuelling trucks 6, 10, 11, 38

safety equipment 28, 29
servicing trucks 10, 11
simulator 35, 39
stack 26, 39

takeoff 17
terminal buildings 6, 8
tickets 9
time zones 34
training 35
turbofan, turbojet 18, 35, 39
turnaround 39

USA 4, 34, 36

V1, V2 decision points 18, 39

winglets 33, 39
World War I 36
Wright brothers 36

x-ray scanners 9, 39

Answers to Tail Quiz, page 6
1 Cyprus Airways
2 Finnair
3 Japan Air lines
4 Lufthansa
5 Air New Zealand
6 Alitalia
7 Aeroflot
8 Air Canada
9 Air France
10 El Al

Answers to Signwriter Quiz, page 32
1 Aeroflot
2 Air France
3 Lufthansa
4 Swissair
5 Japan Air Lines
6 Aer Lingus